FUNDAMENTALS OF URBAN DESIGN

Richard Hedman with Andrew Jaszewski

Planners Press
American Planning Association
Washington, D.C.   Chicago, Illinois

Only the assistance of Sharon Rogers
and Ann Fredricks prevented this project
from falling into the abyss.

All photographs and drawings
are by Andrew Jaszewski unless
otherwise indicated.

Table of Contents

BACKGROUND

Architecture and urban design are frequently discussed as if they had nothing to do with each other when in fact they are inseparable. When we talk about one, we are also talking about the other, conscious of the fact or not. Failure to recognize the linkage between architecture and urban design is to invite confusion if not chaos. Yet each day countless architectural decisions are made with little or no awareness of their urban design consequences. In this day and age, when architecture comes in so many shapes and flavors, this is a high-risk undertaking, and our towns and cities are not better for it.

Everywhere cities, towns, and suburbs find it difficult to secure coherent and satisfying patterns of development. While individual buildings may be attractive or exciting in themselves, the cumulative effect is disappointing. There is no sum of parts adding up to a greater whole. Strong organizing patterns are missing. Exterior spaces around buildings are weak, uneventful, and without clear form or character. Remaining older buildings look like urban

Historic buildings often are treated with all the respect of leftovers. Instead of proud reminders, these small buildings have been transmuted into pitiful remainders.

leftovers: lost, unattached fragments of a now alien past. The net effect at its worst is of a fractured disjointed world of divisions without connecting seams, a world offering residents no identifiable center other than the buildings in which they live.

There are many possible causes for the difficulty communities are encountering in achieving some degree of design coherence. The divisive impact of the auto and the continuing flood of innovations in materials and construction are both obvious factors that immediately come to mind. As important as these issues are, they fail to explain the underlying lack of design order. However, the auto and new building technologies would by their nature amplify and exagerate any fundamental changes in how architects go about designing buildings—and consequently how cities and towns are built.

There was a time not too long ago when architecture seemed to take care of urban design requirements without the need for some kind of urban design overview. There was built-in sensibility that ensured a reasonable degree of order and harmony within the built environment. But that state of affairs has changed to such a degree that architecture often contributes to the disorder and disharmony of the urban environment. Imbedded within contemporary design, there appears to be a strong and virulent strain of antiurbanism. The origins of this negative attitude are to be found in the beginnings of modern architecture.

In the mid-1950s architectural history was presented as a slow, evolutionary process, one style growing from another in small increments. The pendulum moved ever so slowly from the formal to the romantic, then back again for another cleansing dose of classical formality. Architectural history unfolded this way from the earliest structures of Egypt and Crete, and each subsequent architectural phase was firmly rooted in the previous era. Then suddenly and unnaturally, the entire evolutionary process was presented as coming to a shuddering halt early this century. History stopped and modern art and architecture appeared, pure and independent of past history.

Modern art and architecture did not appear suddenly by themselves but were the end product of powerful stresses within society generated by accelerating industrial development and a changing economy. A boiling revolutionary fervor sweeping through the intellectual centers of Europe gave direction to the work of an emerging new generation of artists and architects. Traditional patterns of architecture and city building were viewed by this new

The buildings in the background represent the "outmoded" architecture of the past. To the right stands the "new" architecture, raised off the ground on slender piers and presenting a tight no-nonsense image of structural honesty. While neither stands comfortably next to the other, the new needs the old to help define and enrich the space before it.

generation as synonymous with an oppressive and uncaring society, to be discarded and replaced by new forms based on modern rational and humanistic thinking. A whole new beginning was called for; architects would create a new architecture that would solve the social problems of the cities.

Creating a totally new architecture proved simple once the basic concept was grasped: Do the extreme opposite—in every way—of what prevailed. If windows were vertically shaped openings spaced at intervals along a wall, the new revolutionary window would be a continuous ribbon of glass. If buildings sat in repose on the ground, they were lifted onto columns or nestled into the earth. Where buildings were packed tightly together defining the street with precision, the new world would build freestanding towers in park-like settings. Where turn-of-the-century buildings were piled high with great pastry-chef concoctions, the new architecture would have no ornamentation. Its form would be derived from the internal functional and structural requirements of the building. A rigorous sys-

4

tem of analysis evolved that became a powerful weapon in the rout
of traditional architecture. In the process of rejecting the past, modern architecture became the inversion of past values. The new method of rational (scientific) analysis was and remains an invaluable tool.
The problems that have emerged in subsequent years stem not from
the methodology but the narrowness of its application.

  The modern office building provides an example of the new kind

*The design of this tower ensures
that the tower will never be an integral part of the surrounding city.
The suburban base suggests that it
should not be in a city.*

of architectural thinking. Logically considered, an office building is nothing more than a number of flat floors stacked one on top of the other. The size and shape of the floors is determined by analysis of the potential users' needs and the ease of subdividing the floor space. The shape of the building results from stacking the floors, with the number of floors determined by the size of the budget. The top of the building is flat for the simple reason that a flat roof best expresses the flat floors beneath. The exterior is clad in prefabricated modules of identical size and shape because they are most efficient. There is no rational basis for making one window larger than another. Step-by-step functional logic dictates the parameters of design. The architect merely has to fill in the blanks, and he has the wonder of wonders: the box-top office tower. The problem with the analysis is that it focuses exclusively upon the internal functional concerns and ignores the role of the building in the cityscape or in the definition of street space.

The revolutionary birth of modern architecture has left a lasting imprint upon the architectural profession. The moral disdain early modernists displayed toward traditional styles manifests itself today in the disregard so many architects show for the existing buildings surrounding their projects. The lack of respect for older buildings combined with an emphasis upon an internally focused analysis encourages the design of buildings that relate only to themselves. Revolution has been translated into a kind of ritualistic contrariness; there is constant pressure to be new and different and to visually reject the validity of surrounding development. The net effect is an antiurbanism that is expressed in many subtle and not so subtle design mannerisms, well suited for almost anything but building cities.

In the high excitement of the architectural revolution, when the symbols of an oppressive past were being jettisoned, something else at the heart and soul of urban design that constituted acquired wisdom of great importance was also tossed out. Hidden among the belt courses, capitals, and brackets was a concern for the definition and dramatization of exterior space. Encapsulated within traditional architecture was an attitude toward the street that viewed architectural expression as a form of urban theater. Individual buildings played well-defined parts in a larger drama, subordinating themselves according to the requirements of the role. What was lost was the understanding that *urban design is a function of architecture*.

At the very moment in history when design principles for securing cohesive urban development were needed, they were rejected out-of-hand.

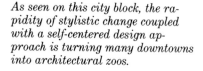

As seen on this city block, the rapidity of stylistic change coupled with a self-centered design approach is turning many downtowns into architectural zoos.

Architecture today is very much a creature of fashion. As neckties widen and narrow and hemlines rise and fall, so architectural enthusiasms crescendo, wane, shift, and change. Where in previous eras the changes were in the detail, now they are in major aspects of form and character. A phenomenal number of stylistic flurries have drifted across the architectural scene during the past 20 years. Such a rapid shift in styles makes the achievement of any sense of cohesiveness, order, and true contrast extremely difficult. Needed are some external constraints that only urban design considerations can supply.

One ray of hope has been a recent interest among a few architects in relating their designs to the contextual setting. Compared with the vast army of architectural rationalists practicing their trade the trend is so miniscule that it could drift off the page of the magazines as quickly as it appeared. To the degree that the new contextualism represents an attempt to contrast and stand out from other contemporary designs, rather than to correct urban design deficiencies, it will be as transitory as other fashion movements.

The nature of the architecture in use at a given place and time dictates the kind of city that can be achieved. A suburban-styled architecture, for example, cannot yield an urban city. The long, low, horizontal lines that characterize most suburban architecture are limited in the kind and size of space they can define effectively. If the work of local architects is wildly dissimilar, achieving any kind of coherent design may be impossible. Architectural characteristics thus have a major impact upon the city that can be built. Failure to respect the limitations of the architecture or to alter its nature is to court disaster. The urban design objectives a community selects for itself contain implicit rules for the architecture required to accomplish them. The planners, urban designers, and city managers who do not understand this cannot defend their communities from well-intentioned—even attractive—but nevertheless damaging projects.

Achieving good urban design does not require that every decision maker becomes skilled in design analysis. It does demand that the people involved in important design decisions know what to look for, the questions to ask, and have at least a rough idea of the criteria to consider. This book is addressed to setting out fundamental directions for achieving a more cohesive and satisfying environment.

CONTEXT and CONTRAST

Couldn't the architect of the building on the left see the fine old bank building across the street? Now the street is divided by an architectural barrier many times stronger than the streetcar (LRV) tracks.

Designing in context means providing enough visual linkages between existing buildings and a proposed project so as to create a cohesive overall effect. The new building should strengthen and enhance the characteristics of its setting, or at least maintain key unifying patterns.

Visual linkages are not mysterious entities that only professionals can understand, but are simple, basic features. Window proportions, entryway placements, decorative elements, style, materials, and silhouette are examples of features that contribute to the sense of unity or disunity of a street, neighborhood, or district. Every place has its own mixture of these elements and level of tolerance for design variety.

Standing Ground

A building need not ape the stylistic mannerisms of its neighbors to fit into its context and support the visual unity of the area; it must, however, share certain fundamental characteristics with them. Contextual design is a useful preservation tool because it allows preserved buildings to be retained within an appropriate and supportive context. In a city with any heritage of well-designed buildings and neighborhoods, the most important action planners and citizens can take is to insist that the architectural designer respect the positive qualities of the existing environment. If the designer presses for an exception to contextual requirements so he can achieve his current manifestation of brilliance, the community is wise to resist the temptation—the successful tour de force is a rare occurrence that requires the right site, a superb designer, an adequate budget, an exceptional client, and a sophisticated and supportive bureaucracy. A community has the right to insist that new buildings respect the scale and character of nearby structures of merit and that they contribute to an overall impression of unity.

The urban areas of this country that possess a strong spirit of unity are rare and endangered. New additions are more likely to look out of place and at odds with their neighbors than to fit comfortably with them. The most satisfying areas are blessed by a pervasive sense of cohesiveness, of buildings working together to create an overall effect greater than the individual parts. Once the unity of an area is damaged by an ill-considered project, decades may pass before the error can be redressed. Once compromised, the area's ability to fend off subsequent attacks upon its design integrity is weakened. A problem shared by all growing cities is the repeated failure of today's designers to consider in their designs the character of the surrounding environment. A consequence is that a new project seldom shares any qualities of neighboring buildings, thereby breaking established patterns that provide visual unity, and causing the failure of buildings to work together toward a common effect. At times, routine indifference turns into a form of active design warfare where the observer might conclude that the designer had utter contempt for all nearby buildings, and while this might be true, it is more than likely that the designer was only trying to make a dramatic statement in the "modern tradition."

The small gestures made on the facade, reflecting the architectural lines of the adjacent building, are insufficient to overcome the extravagant differences. Replacing the Egyptianesque parapet with a bold cornice and the dark vertical window bands with more appropriately proportioned openings would have made a positive linkage.

Contrast can be exciting and is appropriate in some circumstances. Buildings of civic importance are typically set apart by their design and placement to underscore their significance but, as a rule, more common uses such as residential and commercial space are not so distinguished. The practical design reasoning for this is that a few special buildings provide accent and focus, but if all buildings seek to contrast the result is chaos.

People protest when disharmony is glaring and obvious, but otherwise seem to have a high tolerance for lesser conflicts and omissions. This is unfortunate because the cumulative impact of many minor infractions of good urban manners can be as deadly as a single glaring infraction and can affect a larger area. Again, it is important to insist that all new buildings demonstrate due respect and consideration for their context where warranted. This is not something to be done only sometimes or halfway, and it requires the exercise of flexible, yet sensitive, design evaluation and the ability to see the good qualities in all kinds of architecture— independent of the distortions of fashion. If architects cannot or will not provide the guiding vision, then it must come from the design review process.

A single new building or a small number of buildings that support rather than compete with the established character of an area are "good neighbors." They harmonize with the surrounding buildings, avoid disruptive excesses, and do not compete for attention.

Harmony/Disharmony

The seven-story building (center) fits comfortably with its neighbors, continuing the pattern of the bays. The building's height forms an intermediate step between the tall building on the left and the smaller buildings on the right.

Where contrast is introduced, it avoids being abrasive, and seeks civilized liveliness instead. On a street that has a strong character, a new "good neighbor" will not attempt to be the center of attention, but on a dull street it might be appropriate to add a needed visual focus. Every cluster, blockfront, or district of like-minded buildings has its own specific interpretation of the rules for being a good neighbor. For the competent designer, perceiving and following the interpretations required should be neither difficult nor inimical to good design.

Contextual design is rarely a matter of absolutes. In most situations the choices can be made from an array of options that are bracketed between total conformity and maximum contrast. Choosing the correct prescription often involves more common sense than finely tuned design sensitivity. Long-term city planning considerations may also play an important part: Where community policies encourage substantial change, such as a sharp increase in density, then close design adherence to the existing context may not be warranted and the designer may have the opportunity to help establish a new design direction for an area. Conversely, if the community wants to keep an area close to its present appearance, a high degree of conformity is required.

Situational Differences

Decision making is always easier when the choices are etched in sharp contrast; reality is only occasionally cooperative in this regard. A typical situation may require the consideration of planning objectives, economic practicalities, and an existing group of buildings that offer only the most vague directives as to contextual requirements. Under such circumstances precise and rigid requirements would be difficult to defend.

Understanding the nature of the problem is a prerequisite to good urban design analysis. The following categories provide an idea of the variety of possible situations:

Optional

In situations where buildings are visually insulated from each other by dense foliage—such as that found in many suburban locations—wide design variations may occur without damage to the context of other buildings. How the community sees itself may be more important than any real design problem. Areas in transition, where the existing buildings are without merit or are otherwise slated by public policy for massive change, offer the opportunity to create a new context. However, if there are some meritorious qualities that would serve as a benchmark for new development, developing them can help reinforce the community's sense of identity and continuity.

Selective Linkages

Where quality is mixed—good buildings mixed with more mundane construction—a more selective approach may be warranted. Districts with only a mild sense of cohesiveness or a uniformity verging on the bland in some ways are more delicate than the other categories. Identifiable patterns should be reinforced wherever possible and negative design qualities, however much they may characterize an area, should be avoided.

Moderate Conformance

Greater latitude of design response is possible where there is a diversity of style. Those shared characteristics that impart an overall sense of unity and harmony become key ingredients for a compatible design. New elements can be introduced—provided they are accompanied by strong design linkages.

Rigorous Conformance

Districts composed of architecturally significant buildings that share many detail and attitude similarities should not be played with lightly. In such areas, the community will best be served by maintaining those special attributes. This requires buildings that will fit in with great sensitivity. Imitation usually is not necessary, but careful attention to design linkages at all levels is.

Replication

In most cities, replication of adjacent buildings is extremely rare. A vacant site in the middle of what was once a historic row of identical buildings of architectural merit is an example of such a situation. To place in such a site a building of only similar appearance would introduce a false note and detract from the whole because the visual strength of the row is derived from precise repetition.

Replication is easy to understand and request. A city need only direct the developer to make the building look exactly like the one on either side of it—simple and direct. On the other hand, asking a builder to incorporate the shared characteristics that give a group of buildings its sense of cohesiveness requires a detailed understand-

ing of the nature of design linkages and how they work together. A design guide that explains what to look for and gives examples of acceptable solutions to typical problems is a useful document.

Application of Criteria

The row of Queen Anne houses illustrated here provides an excellent starting point for exploring design linkages and application of the criteria. This particular group of row houses combines a powerful sense of unity with considerable design variation. The character of the group is so strong that it is difficult to imagine another type of building inserted into the row without contextual problems. The remarkable design unity of this group is derived from 11 design linkages:

- Building silhouette;

- Spacing between buildings;

- Setbacks from street property line;

- Proportion of windows, bays, doorways, and other features;

- Massing of building form;

- Location and treatment of entryway;

- Surface material, finish and texture;

- Shadow patterns from massing and decorative features;

- Building scale;

- Style of architecture; and

- Landscaping, if any.

The picturesque silhouette of the spiked and turreted towers and steep complex roof forms are the most eye-catching features here. The configuration of each roof varies, yet they are united by similar pitch and scale. The imagery is distinctive.

The spacing and rhythm of this row is established by the spacing of the street facades. The deep notch between the facades creates a pattern of vertical shadow lines framing each frontage and sets the row off from the more typical rowhouse arrangement.

The sense of depth and solidity these Queen Anne homes convey is created by setting the primary facade plane back from the property line to provide space for the large bays. The projections are enhanced by secondary setbacks defining the entryways and the notches between buildings.

16

Windows, doorways, bays, and pediments of these homes share similar proportions that link the buildings although each is composed differently. The different designs also share a common approach: Each is an arrangement of vertical elements tied together in horizontal bands.

Complex solid geometry characterizes this row. Cylinders merge into the building's basic mass and penetrate the triangular roof forms, and bays expand outward in counterpoint to deep recesses carved out of the central mass. The bold manipulation of forms results in buildings with a remarkable sense of volume and mass for their size. Each variation is arrived at out of a juggling of similar-sized components.

How and where a building is entered is usually an important part of the design, and when entryways share common qualities, as these do, they become important design linkages. Each entryway is raised, featuring a stairway framed by bold balustrades leading to a deeply recessed entry or porch.

Exuberantly applied wood moldings, inset panels, brackets, finials, keystones, and decorative shingles cover everything but a few small areas of narrow wood siding. All is carefully covered with paint from top to bottom. The effect is of complexity and richness of detail that enhances the monumental effect of the building forms.

How sunlight and shadow play across a building facade can be just as important as more permanent and tangible features. A complex combination of bold and delicate shadow patterns characterizes this row of Queen Anne row houses.

At first glance this row appears to be of uniform height, but some buildings are a full floor higher than others. The differences are masked by the configuration of the building form. The similarity of height plays an important role in linking these buildings even though it is not rigidly applied.

In this analysis of the Queen Anne rowhouses, 11 aspects of the row that served to link the buildings were identified. There is no particular magic in 11 criteria; the intent was to illustrate an approach. (For instance, the final linkage noted here is the landscaping, which in this case does not exist as the houses start abruptly at the sidewalk. In a suburban situation, however, landscaping could be so important as to be the source of several linkages.) The criteria used for an analysis should grow out of the facts and not depend upon a preordained list.

The validity of a set of criteria can be tested with a design that deliberately ignores or inverts the standards. In the sketch here, each of the linking qualities that characterized the Queen Anne row has been inverted. The unhappy results should be obvious to even the most graphically deprived observer: instead of a peaked roof with conical tower the silhouette is completely flat, the rhythm of closely spaced buildings is broken by its extra width, and built right to the property line the building does not share the setback. The low wide windows could not be more at odds with the tall narrow windows of the row houses, while the doorway opens flatly to the street instead of by a stairway and recessed entry. Compared with the sculptured Queen Anne facades, the front wall of the low building is flat. The unpainted concrete block, stained plywood panels, and the plain trim have no relationship to the elaborate painted woodwork of the townhouses, and the low building's single horizontal shadow line underscores the differences with the elaborate shadow patterns of its much taller neighbors.

Finally, there is the contrasting message of style. The fanciful forms of the Queen Anne homes, with their allusions to the abodes

of ancient noblemen, have nothing in common with the efficient, budget-minded construction of the ranch-style building in the middle. It not only fails to relate in any way with its tall neighbors, it is at war with them. Real life counterparts are not hard to find.

These Queen Anne rowhouses are an extreme example where the issues are clear cut; in most cases, the problems are apt to be more subtle, the issues more difficult to define, and the decision harder to make. What does one do when the proposal meets seven of the 11 criteria and violates the other four? Where is the line drawn? The criteria will not make the decision, but they will help decision makers focus on the essential qualities needed to evaluate a proposal and communicate them to the designer. The weight given to a specific criterion may be expected to vary with the contextual situation and depend on how well the other criteria are met. In the final analysis, it is the overall effect that counts.

Caveats

The checklist is useful in identifying what is wrong and is a resource for determining what should be done to correct the problems. The low building that did nothing right in the Queen Anne rowhouse example might at the very least have been required to be a more tolerable intrusion if conservation of the area's architectural character was a community concern.

The weakness of any checklist or the criteria arrived at through its application lies in the problem of accurately communicating what is expected. Verbally transmitted design directions are notoriously unreliable. The same words can hold radically different meanings for different people and there will always be those who will interpret the words in the narrowest possible sense. A request that the designer respect important building lines of adjacent buildings, made with the objective of realizing a design response of equal strength, might elicit, for example, a single fine line on the facade, noticeable to only the most perceptive observer. Communication problems of this kind can be avoided if designers can be referred to sites where the criterion has been successfully applied. Graphic notations should also be used to more accurately convey design ideas.

Today's Challenges

The insertion of new, large, high-rise towers among older, relatively small-scaled commercial buildings is a problem many cities share. Suburban areas may be able to obliterate the problem by packing the spaces between large and small buildings with a little more green stuff, but in urban settings where both buildings may share a property line, the juxtaposition of large and small forms can be disconcerting. A small building—however excellent its architecture—can appear as an awkward leftover someone forgot to remove. A community can secure preservation of a notable building and simultaneously negate its urban value by permitting an overscaled high rise to loom over it. The problem, however, is much greater than the occasional bullying of a landmark. Large high-rise buildings and lower, but huge, buildings have demonstrated the capacity to overwhelm entire blocks and break urban areas into disconnected fragments.

Abrupt and excessive difference in scale can be minimized, if not eliminated, by creating transitional or intermediate scaled steps between the low buildings and the high or large buildings. The lowest of the steps should be within a comfortable scale range of the small building, generally within two and one half times its height.

In some locations it may be important to minimize the impact of even fairly modest departures of scale, such as in a historic district composed of predominately two-and three-story buildings. Since, in terms of visual context, what can be seen is the issue and that

A tall building can easily overwhelm a small neighbor when the taller building lacks scale-giving features and provides no design linkages to the small building.

Creating transitional scaled steps in the larger building is one way of providing a setting for the small building respectful of its smaller size.

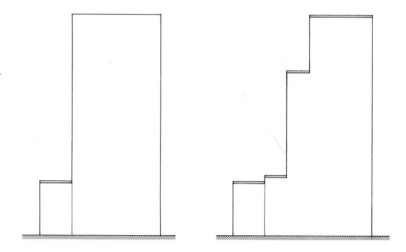

which cannot be seen is irrelevant, a simple solution is to let the potential unseen volume define the permitted building envelope.

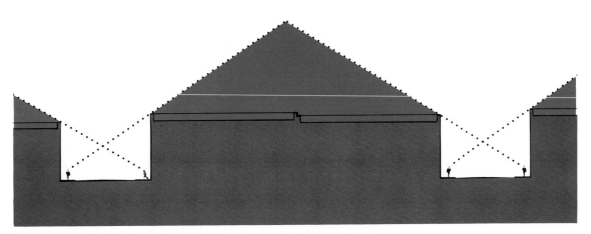

There are parts of most cities—sometimes rather large parts—that essentially have no context as has been discussed here. Remnants of the past have been eradicated; remaining buildings are of no structural, aesthetic, or historical consequence or the land is a blank slate waiting for the first impression. Probably the most common approach is to let the first project proposed establish the frame of reference. When lucky, the approach works and requires the least effort.

Occasionally a community will try design guidelines, and with luck they sometimes prove effective. A problem with design guidelines arises when they are in the form of verbal injunctions, heavily larded with good intentions. When it comes to design, words are notoriously slippery and a verbally adroit person can be remarkably evasive. Before an audience of nondesigners, it is easy to make the thinnest token gestures seem to fully meet the criteria.

The dotted lines define the volume wherein additional building mass would not be visible from the public right-of-way.

As an alternate approach, a community might create an *elective* context composed of drawings and/or photographs of different groups of buildings to serve as the model context for design purposes. Even inexperienced nondesigners can effectively judge how the designs relate in this theoretical context. A model context could be a good way to achieve some sense of unity where several independent projects are in progress. This technique is not too much different than what happens in the drafting room of architectural/design offices, where instead of a selection of buildings chosen by the community's representatives they are looking at the latest issue of *Progressive Architecture* or other trade magazines.

A similar approach can be applied to mixed quality areas, where good buildings are intermixed with less desirable structures. In such a case, buildings that should serve as context to be related to and those that may be ignored can be specified.

EFFECTIVE CONTRAST

The contrast between these two buildings is dramatic and visually satisfying—within the frame of this photograph. But reality is another matter; it has no neat frame and involves much more than differences of texture and pattern. Streets become schizophrenic casualties of the never-ending design warfare.

Contrast is essential to creating a lively and interesting urban environment, but like any strong seasoning it must be used sparingly and with great care. Contrast is one of the most powerful design tools available to the designer. Used wisely it can provide focus and great drama to areas of the city; used carelessly it will self-destruct, transforming order into chaos. During the 1960s and 1970s, contrast was overused and abused. Its effects have been destructive at times, yet it has a legitimate role in urban design and valuable gifts to offer. Understanding its nature and limitations is the key to making it work for rather than against cities and towns.

The radically new and different building stands in dramatic contrast to its neighboring structures.

When joined by another contrasting building, the cohesive frame of ornate buildings begins to erode.

Now the radically different building is the last of the original structures.

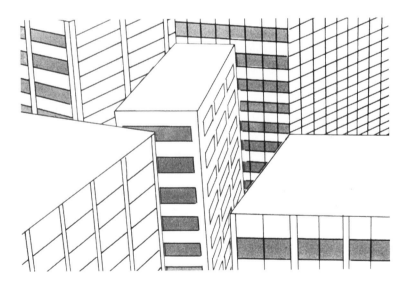

All older buildings are gone; the new architecture has nothing with which to contrast and the drama has vanished.

Perceptions of Quality

What might have been considered a jarring clash of competing styles and forms a century ago appears tame and well-mannered to modern eyes. The intervening years have seen a steady erosion of the constraints that guide the actions of architects. Today, an architect who does not seek to position himself on the frontier of architectural style is not considered very creative. The perception is that the more his work differs from his compatriots, the more likely it is that someday he will be recognized as a daring innovative designer and his designs will appear on the covers of magazines. Modern architecture emphasizes revolutionary change, not the ever-so-slow design evolution that marked earlier eras. A common belief is that the greatest architects are those who break the most rules and trash the past most thoroughly. The public has bought this idea and is now more than ever fascinated with the new and radically different—irrespective of the effect upon the cityscape. The problems this creates in realizing a coherent urban design are monumental.

Part of the problem is at the university level where, instead of providing continuity and a thoughtful overview, many faculty are caught up in the same single-minded search for the new and different. Every school has its would-be architectural "revolutionary" seeking a fast media ride to fame and fortune in the outside world. The motivation to come up with a daring new design direction is imbedded in the present crop of practicing architects, and their future replacements show only the spottiest likelihood of being any different. There is a glimmer of hope in that "contextualism" is one of the current trends. Whether it will become a permanent part of architecture or be another passing fad has yet to be determined.

Use of Contrast

Given the architectural environment, it is the urban designer's task to guide and direct the use of contrast. Unlike the concept of identicality, architectural contrast is not a neat, precisely defined compartment. It starts somewhere short of absolute replication and shifts in infinite graduations into ever wilder permutations. Contrast can be achieved in as many ways as there are degrees of intensity. Color, texture, form, style, structure, and materials can each be carried to the wildest extreme or combined in an unexpected way. A building can be made so brilliantly colorful that all others appear pale and bland, so acrobatic in its structural gyrations that its neighbors seem earthbound and weak, or so resolutely urban that its suburban neighbors appear sadly out of place. The means elected

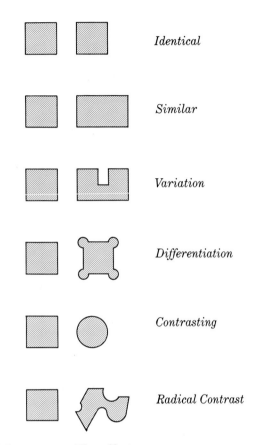

Identical

Similar

Variation

Differentiation

Contrasting

Radical Contrast

for achieving contrast affect the nature of the contrast. The effect can be positive, such as providing a needed focus or climax to a cluster of buildings, or it can be destructive, such as destroying carefully and delicately wrought linkages uniting a whole.

There are so many variations and potential situations that hard and fast rules guiding the use of contrast are impossible. The decision involves the interaction of a multitude of design factors—whether or not the decision maker is aware of them. An aesthetic judgement call is always involved: Someone must determine if the proposed construction is of intrinsic merit, is of vulgar and cheap showmanship, or is so aggressively at war with the world around it that it never will be a comfortable part of its setting.

Observations

Assuming that negative, destructive kinds of contrast are excluded, there are some useful observations regarding contrast's *nature* that can help in arriving at sound conclusions. These deal mainly with the situation, rather than details, of the problem.

The State of Illinois Center may pretend to be a sculpture, but its real intent is to grab attention to itself. The size and placement of the building make it a divisive and destructive entity within its context.

SR: Your buildings give off a tremendous sense of energy. HJ: They (my buildings) are intended to be objects rather than the historic principle of building in a city with common facades. There's a belief that in our time we don't have the uniformity of style anymore; we don't have a uniformity of thinking. So it is the objects which create the context of the city, rather than the spaces in between those buildings.—Helmut Jahn in interview by Sugar Rautbord for Interview Magazine, *September, 1983.*

Photograph by Ron Gordon.

Community Size

The tolerance for contrast varies directly with a community's size. A small New England village has virtually no room for radical contrast on a building scale. A minor degree of contrast in such a setting is acceptable when there is a strong skein of design linkages tying the parts together—the church may have a steeple that sets it apart, but the clapboard siding and all the qualities it shares with the other buildings in the community more than compensate for its

A modern sculpture viewed against a backdrop of ornamented buildings provides an exciting and enjoyable counterpoint. Each enhances the other. The cube neither competes directly with the background buildings nor interrupts their integrity of effect. The adjacent building is another matter.

unique qualities. Small contrasting objects such as a statue or monument are eminently acceptable since they do not upset the balance. It requires a certain critical mass to tolerate larger and stronger forms of contrast. Big cities such as Chicago or New York can tolerate numerous contrasting stuctures without apparent damage as long as the buildings are well isolated from each other and play a positive role in their individual settings.

Discordance

When every building seeks to be the center of attention, a novel and unique architectural statement unto itself, the buildings combine

The unity of Santa Rosa, California's courthouse square area has been carelessly weakened by several buildings that ignore their setting and rudely go their own way.

to an unexpected effect. Instead of providing an exciting counterpoint, the addition of each new and different building intensifies the impression of a nervous, irritating confusion. As more and more of the city is composed of unrelated bits and pieces, it becomes increasingly difficult to make rhyme or reason out of the resulting pattern. The fragmenting effect of excessive contrast is most apparent in urban settings, and while the wrapping of trees and green stuff makes it less obvious in suburban locations, excessive contrast remains a baleful influence on the environment.

Successful, positive use of contrast is guided by basic rules governing size and placement. A contrasting building should never be treat-

Contrasting buildings that fight each other as well as the surrounding context should be visually isolated from each other.

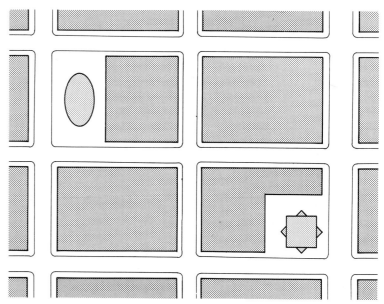

ed as just another building because it is special in nature and demands a different setting. Highly energetic buildings are appreciated best within a frame of quiet orderly construction, much as abstract art appears at its best in a serene museumlike setting. Where there are two or more unrelated contrasting buildings, they should be visually isolated from each other in both close and distant views. Contrasting buildings that share an evident design link-

Limiting highly contrasting buildings to a sharply delineated district is one possible way of minimizing their potential disruptive impact on the cityscape, by transforming them from discordant random events into a planned special place.

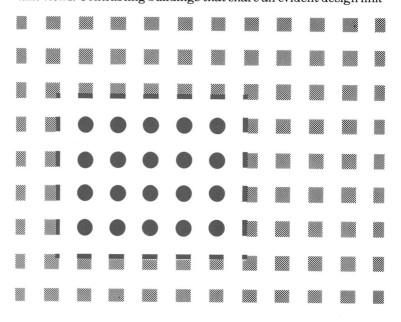

age might be clustered to form a distinctive architectural district. A frame that formally recognizes the perimeter of such a district will help integrate the district into the city.

A contrasting building placed so that it will be seen in close proximity with other buildings that constitute its setting should share sufficient design linkages with them to offset those aspects that set it apart. In the absence of any shared qualities, the contrasting building should be separated from adjacent buildings or otherwise made to appear to be disengaged from its background. The larger the building and the stronger the contrast, the larger the frame of space needed. Conversely, much larger buildings might sucessfully encyst a very small contrasting building.

There are many valuable services that contrast can legitimately perform: announcing the importance of a socially significant use, providing a central focus to a large open space, giving needed accent to excessively uninteresting areas, or introducing a larger order into the cityscape to help define neighborhoods and districts and to help clarify visually how the community is organized. But there should be a clear and compelling urban design reason for introducing a high degree of contrast into any area. It is the random, meaningless dispersal of contrast in the city that is most disturbing. This contrast has nothing to do with the order of the city and everything to do with the spastic contortions of architectural and mercantile egos. Extreme contrast is a dangerous luxury unessential for the creation of variety or delight.

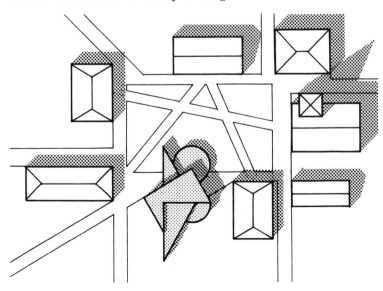

The highly contrasting building in this cluster of buildings is sited in the same manner as its neighbors. By its nature it is attacking the fundamental order of the entire complex and through the use of destructive contrast claims supremacy for itself.

Suburban development often suffers from an excessive monotony that comes in part from the ever-present greenery and the uniform lowness of most buildings. The injection of small doses of urbanity at key points is a possible method for creating a more decisive impression of order.

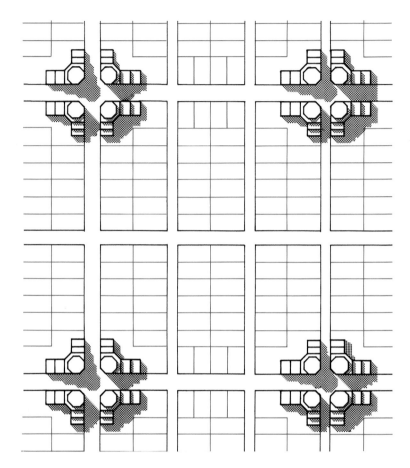

PRESERVATION

Older buildings contribute a richness of form, detail and texture to the cityscape that most contemporary buildings lack. Photographer: Malcolm Lubliner

Cities are improved over time by replacing bad architecture with good and by protecting structures of merit. Urban design problems begin when cities routinely allow mediocre buildings to replace better buildings. Saving older buildings of merit is much more than an exercise in nostalgia because such buildings provide a sense of continuity and are an irreplaceable record of changing vision and values. Their continued presence adds to the complexity and richness of any city or town. The very best buildings serve as benchmarks by which a community can measure the value of proposed new additions to its building stock.

Preservation is an essential part of urban design, and good urban design would be virtually impossible to sustain without it.

Most building design predating the modernist movement adheres to an important set of traditions governing how a building should address the street. As no accepted and workable set of alternatives to these traditions has evolved, such buildings become key building blocks for achieving good urban design. They provide a cohesive strength lacking in much contemporary design and establish an orderly framework for future development.

Few people are against the general objectives of preservation however strenuously some may object when personally affected. Beautiful old homes, neighborhoods, and towns are widely cherished and admired, and in the past 10 years public support for preservation has grown phenomenally. Preservation organizations formerly con-

Tradition and Design

I.M. Pei's plan for Society Hill in Philadelphia replaced these buildings that followed Canal Street's lazy reverse "S" curve with a grid-iron pattern of development.

cerned with the creation of museums and encouraging individual efforts with little voice in community affairs have now become influential advisory groups.

The rising public concern about preservation is a reaction to the rapidity and magnitude of change that has occurred over the past quarter century. During that period, a continental freeway system was superimposed on cities, towns, and farmlands. The freeways were followed by mile after mile of suburban tract homes which in turn altered patterns of home and work. Downtowns first were gutted by an explosion of parking lots, then invaded by remote and alien buildings that steadfastly ignored the fragments of the past that surrounded them. These physical changes were accompanied by equally disruptive social changes. Overwhelmed by the progress they once eagerly anticipated, many people sought escape in a more peaceful milieu. The faded signs on old brick walls that were symbols of economic stagnation in the 1930s became memento mori of a long lost innocent age. Initially attracted by the warmth and security of an unchanging past, many rediscovered the value of history, continuity, and tradition. The growth of the preservation movement owes much to this change of public attitude. The tragedy is that it has taken so long to reach its present strength and that so many irreplaceable buildings have been lost along the way.

Uneven Progress

The increased strength of the national preservation movement has not been accompanied by a matching increase of preservation powers in all cities. In many communities the starting point has been so low that preservation's recent growth still leaves it in a marginal position—the preservation groups are just not losing as often. Until preservation occupies a more assured position within local government, preservationists will be forced to accept compromises of one sort or another. Entry into city hall will become easier as more preservationists learn to shed some of their militant rigidity and negotiate more effectively. A few bright resourceful preservationists are aware of this, but their freedom to negotiate is limited by the emotional absolutism of their membership.

Preservation is not a simple endeavor with a single clear-cut objective. It is complicated in the many layers of historical reality and contradiction because traces of other phases of history are often eradicated in the process of preserving a selected part of history. A major national effort has been made to set forth guidelines and rules to minimize contradictions and discourage practices now considered unsound. How durable these guidelines prove to be will depend on how well they adapt to a wide range of unique situatons. Quite rightly, preservationists fear undisciplined actions they may not be able to control, but as the number of buildings under preservation control and the variety of situations increase, too inflexible an approach may be difficult and even unwise to sustain.

The efforts of local preservation groups to save individual historically significant structures contrast with the large scale efforts by the National Park Service and private philanthropists to recreate entire villages and settlements representative of important phases of American history. Neither approach, characterized by differing objectives and methodology, has ever rested comfortably with the other or fully resolved their differences. Nor does either approach provide a guide particularly applicable to the urban commercial situations into which preservation is moving.

Everyone would agree that the reroofing and painting of an eighteenth century home falls within the bounds of preservation as actions essential to maintaining the building over time and falling within normal maintenance activity. As the amount of damaged or worn material requiring replacement increases, a point is eventually reached where there is so much more replacement than preservation that the end product might more properly be termed reconstruction instead of preservation. The problem of definition is that there are no clear-cut break points dividing the activities falling along the continuum between preservation and recontruction under the name of restoration.

**Preservation/
Reconstruction**

Preservation ◄ Restoration ► Reconstruction

In the past, "historical" buildings have been recreated from little more than a bit of lead guttering and a few foundation stones. Projects have required that architecturally and historically significant buildings be demolished to return an area to its appearance at a given point in time, eliminating all evidence of subsequent history. Reconstruction is now opposed by many preservationists as false and dishonest while restoration, by and large, remains a widely accepted activity, even though what goes on behind the scaffolding is often remarkably difficult to distinguish from reconstruction. A building is often so peeled apart in the restoration process that little remains but portions of the structural shell—the difference be-

In returning the area around Independence Hall to its appearance at a specific time in history, this bank building by Frank Furness was demolished.

tween restoration and recreation may be little more than the use of some of the original trim. It could be argued that the only effective difference is knowledge: If the viewer doesn't know new material was largely used he might think it a marvel that an old building could survive in such fine condition. How much of a building must be torn down to be considered demolished or how much must be retained to be called restored remains a troublesome question at the very core of preservation.

Realities and Ironies

If the place where Jefferson penned some of his more important thoughts is the building in question, then the fact that the floor was the very one he trod upon and the walls and windows the very ones he looked at serves to make history live as no reconstruction could. But what about architectural preservation, where only the exterior will be maintained in its original form? How important is the use of original material to the appreciation of architecture? Architecture, unlike a historic event, can be accurately measured and recreat-

ed. When the Gold Pavilion (Kinkakuji) in Kyoto was burned down by an unhappy citizen following World War II, the Japanese government rebuilt the pavilion from careful measurements made before the war. It is no less a beautiful moving spectacle when viewed at sunset across the shadowed waters of the pond than if centures old. Did the Japanese err in recreating a national treasure when nothing of the old except the design was used, or is our "save every brick" approach too doctrinaire in such situations?

Along with reconstruction, the once busy activity of moving historic buildings from their original locations has now fallen out of favor. Lifting a building from where it was built seems to isolate a building from reality and its linkage with history, and somehow makes it less real in the eyes of many observers. The irony here is that if the building had been moved to a different site a long time ago, the building's importance would be enhanced. If the name of the man who had the house moved is known, such as "Captain Isiah Smith had the house moved to its present location in 1868 as a wedding present to his daughter...," the event is personalized and the significance may be doubly enhanced. The same beneficial effect of time applies to remodeling as well. If the remodeling or addition was done in the distant past, it has a good chance of becoming a valued part of the building's pedigree. However, should someone in many cities today attempt to move or remodel a historic building, he should expect to be unceremoniously ushered out of town.

Another irony of preservation is that the more accurately a build-

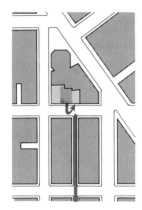

View axis down Maiden Lane from Union Square.

The small building, to the right of the tower, was proposed to be demolished by the developer. When San Francisco made clear that it did not want to lose the ornate Maskey Building, the architect proposed moving the building and modifying the width of the project so that it symmetrically terminated the view down Maiden Lane from Union Square in San Francisco. Located in this precise place, the building will permit a future mid-block passage to a plaza on the opposite side of the block.

ing and its furnishings are returned to a particular point in time, the more it becomes a form of theater. It may be very subtle and refined or insufferably cute, but it is theater to the extent that it is a staging of the past. In opposition to this approach, there are those who assert that the truest expression of history is to be found in the unrestored building, be it intact or a shambling wreck. There is much truth in this idea, but it has the disadvantage of rendering much of our heritage inaccessible. At the center of these and related issues is the concern for maintaining a building's connection to history, a concern that surfaces with each effort to infuse old buildings with new life.

Richardson's Trinity Church was not destroyed with the building of I.M. Pei's Hancock Building, but its context was severely damaged. The buildings repel each other like the identical poles of magnets.

"Good/Bad" Preservation

Thoughtful preservationists will be debating what is and is not good preservation for some time. The shift of the preservation focus from the creation of Williamsburgs, historic districts, and mansions to the central business districts will necessarily contribute new dimensions to that discussion, and that is where urban design considerations also come into play. Preservationists can be so concerned with the saving of a building that they ignore existing or potential contextual problems—it is possible to save a building in a situation so at odds with its scale and character that the effect is more a cruel joke than salvation.

The act of saving sets up contextual requirements that must somehow be integrated with the other developmental objectives of the area. Within a historic district or any relatively static low-density area, this may be easy to accomplish, but within a dynamic downtown preservation competes with the private market for the control of land endowed with a potential for extremely intensive use. Saving a building is one thing, but placing limits on the surrounding property in order to maintain an appropriate scaled context is

A more hospitable context is assured by shifting the unused potential floor area to more distant development sites from the vicinity of buildings to be conserved so their small scale will not be overwhelmed.

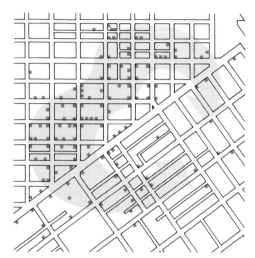

an altogether different problem. To accomplish this, preservation planning must be integrated with city planning and urban design.

The Transfer of Development Rights (TDR) can ease property owner resistance to preservation, but it will not ease the contextual problems of smaller buildings unless the development rights are shifted well away from the buildings being preserved. There are also design alternatives to the massive reduction of development that in many instances will solve these contextual problems. Except for a few very special cases where strong public sentiment may rule, these alternative design maneuvers will most likely be the practical response of elected officials because they do not involve extreme and politically dangerous actions.

In the name of preservation, architects and developers of downtown projects have made some unusual and sometimes bizarre gestures toward "saving" architecturally significant buildings. Facades have had their bodies peeled away and have been left standing like tombstones or grafted onto the skin of a new and much larger host. Small buildings have been straddled by giant office towers or been absorbed in one way or another into their bases, have supported unplanned vertical additions, and have been transmuted into entirely new creations. These various manifestations are all the consequence of preservation pressure to save our architectural heritage.

For the most part, these efforts fall far short of what preservationists wanted to achieve and are far more than what developers wanted to do. They are the kind of compromises that make neither party happy, and the irony is that in 50 to 100 years they may be

One of the older and oddest additions to an existing building is the Custom House Tower in Boston. The addition is picturesque and now old enough to qualify for the benediction of preservationists.

The Old Sub-Treasury in San Francisco was saved in its entirety by bridging the office tower over it. Only the supporting frame of small buildings saves the Sub-Treasury from appearing like a small curious drawer at the base of the high rise. Retention of the scale of building along the alleyway is essential if the effect is not to become bizarre.

San Francisco's struggle to save a fine old banking temple resulted in the developer finally agreeing to save three of the building's five original bays. The temple will be transformed into a glass roofed pavilion. The arched windows have been opened to the ground, offering views and access into the land-scaped inner court. The rich exterior has been saved and the interior exchanged for what should prove an important public amenity.

considered gems of their kind and be valued by future preserva-tionists. Although preservation aberrations by almost any defini-tion, they are not always without merit. They are successful to the degree they contribute to the visual richness of the street, force a more urban response from designers who have a suburban stylis-tic bent, or avoid the bland repetition that passes for modern de-sign. When the changes enhance the visual importance of the retained building or make the architecture more accessible to the public, then the city, although it may be losing some attributes may also gain other values. That there are positive byproducts from these preservation permutations should not be construed to mean that cities would benefit from an endless supply of such oddities. That

An earnest effort was made to re-late the new office tower to the ex-isting banking temple. The ribbing on the spandrel panels matches the fluting on the columns, but the horizontal window bands and the extremely low base height are at complete odds with the proportions of the temple.

The developer wanted to add two stories on top of a three-story building that played a positive supportive role within the streetscape. The effect would have been top heavy and awkward. As there were no preservation restraints upon the building, the solution was to stretch the original facade an extra floor in height. In the process the contextual fit was improved, the facade composition became more graceful, and the obvious addition took on the character of a modest penthouse. This is not preservation with a capital P, but for minor contributory buildings this kind of flexibility is reasonable. Photograph provided by Backen, Arrigoni, and Ross Architects.

The four architecturally significant corner buildings (shaded) have been saved by locating the office-residential tower in the center of the block. The corner buildings buffer surrounding small buildings from the new tower's large bulk and provide the project with an instant base. Illustration provided by Skidmore, Owings, and Merrill, Architects.

46

This row of historic buildings in Washington D.C. was saved from demolition by shortening the length of the buildings and slipping the office slab in behind them. The strong linear form and monolithic character of the office building give it the appearance of an ocean liner slicing through the cityscape.

The linear thrust of this office building is at odds with the rhythm of the small buildings along the street frontage.

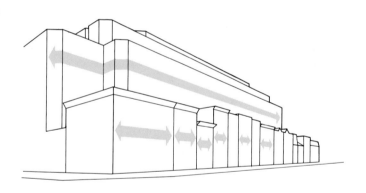

Breaking the slab into form elements similar to the rhythm of the historic row makes the mass far more sympathetic to the scale and character of the retained street frontage.

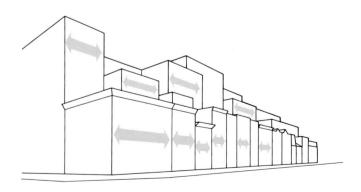

would soon result in a preservation sideshow. A few such exercises in historical integration, if very well done, may find an appropriate place in downtown areas that are already so fractured by new development that a hospitable setting for more ideal preservation is not a realistic objective.

It is difficult to convince officials that it is worth saving a complete row-style commercial building. Consider as an example a good but not outstanding building on the edge of a cluster of such buildings. Blank brick sidewalls stretch back 100 feet and the interior, as is often but not always the case, is profoundly unremarkable. Efforts to designate the building a landmark started only after the building was threatened. (The threat of demolition has a remarkable effect upon how we look at and respond to buildings, they suddenly seem to bloom with qualities no one had observed before, and their previously assigned value may with equal suddenness seem too low.) Convincing planning commissioners, supervisors, and senior bureaucrats that the entire shoebox must be saved is another matter. The developer has reason on his side when he points out that retailing has changed, that deep narrow retail space does not work well, and that few businessmen want light-well office space with too many columns. The developer naturally wants to avoid the expense of dealing with an old building with unknown structural problems and the difficulty of bringing it up to code and integrating it with new construction. He would like to tear the entire thing down and start from scratch, but to avoid further delay he is willing to save the first 15 feet.

Application Problems

The historic or architectural value of saving long blank interior sidewalls that will be largely hidden by adjacent buildings is difficult for many people to understand.

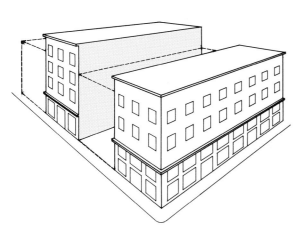

Existing condition, a deep, narrow commercial building.

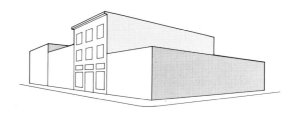

A shortened building of this length still appears very real and practical.

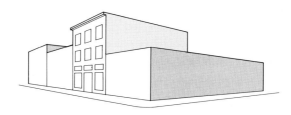

Buildings of these proportions are occasionally seen.

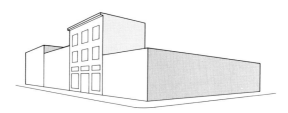

Thicker than a facade but not deep enough to suggest a real building, this looks patently false.

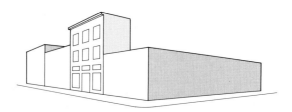

At this point the hunger for new development in the community, the demand for additional commercial space, the amount of extra costs the project can tolerate, and the tradition of preservation concern and action within the community will all affect the politics of the decision-making process. If these factors are tilted against retention and there is no legal protection in place, even a hard-fighting preservation organization would need divine intervention to succeed.

If, after due consideration, the decision makers have indicated that they will support some preservation but are unwilling to go all the way and block the project, some sort of compromise may be the only alternative. Compromise is a rather vague term that could cover a multitude of possibilities up to but not including total demolition. In such a predicament, standards are a useful device for preventing a mockery of both preservation and urban design. It is often here that the urban designer must function as midwife to the birth of the hybrid. Following are some criteria, principles, and observations that may prove useful in articulating some minimum standards when the ideal is out of reach:

- Never reduce the length of a building so much that it loses the appearance of viability, i.e., the building retains the impression of being capable of independent use and appears structurally stable.

- Surrounding buildings should create an appropriately scaled setting that does not overwhelm or otherwise diminish the building's original streetscape role.

- Additions on the tops of buildings should not deform or adversely affect the composition of the facade, nor should the addition be out of scale with the building.

- Reduction of building width may be a possible, if drastic, alternative to total loss if the resultant building appears stable and complete after the architectural amputation. A strong supporting context is crucial when this is attempted.

- Relocation of a structure may be considered if the move places the building in a more compatible and hospitable setting that cannot be achieved on site and/or helps to achieve other desirable design objectives.

- Cantilevering or bridging over a smaller building generally should be avoided because of the bizarre contextual situation in which the

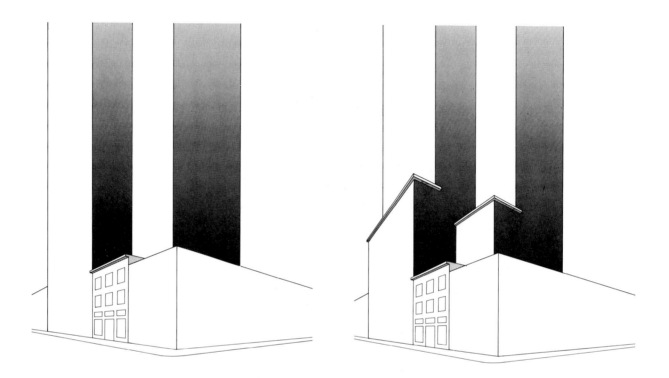

The small building is overwhelmed by its giant neighbor. They stand together like a mouse and a whale.

The introduction of transitional steps in the larger building help place the small building in a more compatible setting.

smaller building is placed. The scale differential tends to turn the smaller building into some kind of relic or curiosity. If the structural overhang can be done unobtrusively or the small building remains firmly connected to a similar scaled context, it may prove worth considering.

Compromise is a poor substitute for a thoughtful preservation program. Sometimes the results are exciting, even excellent, but if continued to excess, the aggregate of all the compromises may result in a surrealistic effect.

The urban designer's motives for preservation may be quite different from those of the preservationist. The building's contribution to the streetscape and the discipline preservation imposes upon abutting new construction may be more important to the urban designer than the building's age and pedigree. Were the choice between saving two complete buildings or six contiguous frontages in a complementary setting, preservationists would be more likely to opt for the first choice and urban designers for the latter. Working out differences of this kind is necessary to avoid the erosion of

Office towers rise with indifference to the Old State House in Boston.

both positions. Activities in both preservation and urban design need each other's support. Urban designers must understand the objective of the preservation movement, and, in turn, preservationists must realize the importance of urban design to preservation and the building of cities.

SPATIAL DEFINITION

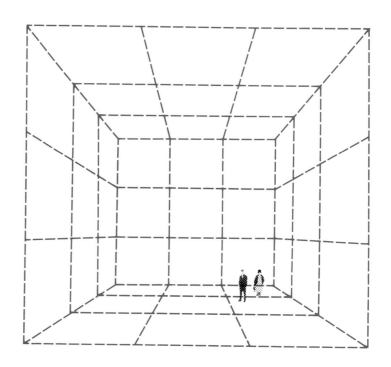

Space is an exceedingly common commodity: It fills the universe and surrounds us throughout our lives. It can appear so thin and extended that the sense of dimension is numbed or so richly infused with a three-dimensional presence that it endows everything within its fold with special meaning. Intensely three-dimensional space has the remarkable capacity to enhance our lives. It imparts our surroundings with a pleasing sense of comfort and security that is as important to the enjoyment of life as sunlight and a place to rest. It is a basic component of good urban design.

However, what is and is not urban design has been the subject of an ongoing scholarly debate. Of basic agreement among contending definitions is the concern of the urban designer with the spaces between buildings. In the narrowest sense this could be concern for the treatment of the sidewalk, street, landscaping, or other areas located between buildings. In this case, the urban designer would be interested in maximizing the area's value as an urban amenity for public enjoyment and would address issues such as adequate seating, the amount of sunlight during hours of maximum potential use, or the need to provide protective measures because of local wind conditions. The height of adjacent buildings would be a concern due to their effect on sunlight, as would the character of ground floor uses because of their impact on the liveliness and usability of the space. If the quality of three-dimensional space and not just the functional use of the ground surface becomes important, then the designer's concern graduates to an entirely different level that involves the architectural characteristics of the building facades and how they work to create a three-dimensional sense of space. This additional concern transforms the problem from landscape architecture to urban design.

POSITIVE SPACE

Among the most accomplished man-made spatial creations in the world are the Renaissance plazas of Italy. For centuries the unique experience they offer has attracted visitors from around the world. Entering one of these places for the first time is a remarkable sensation; the feeling is almost as if the visitor has accidentally stepped onto a great stage where every gesture suddenly becomes important. The atmosphere seems palpable, as if it has to be pushed aside in order to cross the pavement. Curiously, the buildings that create the space seem ancillary to a space that has become a separate entity.

Such intense three-dimensional space offers a positive sensory

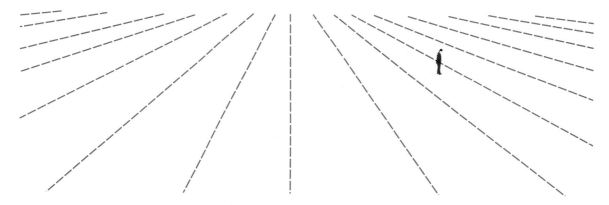

experience that enhances the perception of self by giving each movement special significance. It has the complementary effect of enhancing the perception of community among those sharing the
space through the heightened awareness of their physical relationship to others. When a space possesses this rare and magical quality, designer busywork isn't needed to fill the void. There is no void;
it is filled with positive space.

Comparing three-dimensional space with dimensionless space
helps underscore the point. On the vast plains of the Southwest
where space seems to have no dimension at all, it is possible for a
person to walk for miles yet visually perceive no significant change
and feel that he has made no progress. In the face of such overwhelming distances man is reduced to a marginal entity whose fragile position in the universe is laid bare. Most of the time people dwell
in neither an extremely positive nor negative space, but rather in
a middle world where spaces are not so dimensionless as to repress
or so richly defined as to be noteworthy or exciting.

Out of the miles of new streets built here and abroad, out of the
thousands of new buildings, out of numerous serious efforts to create plazas of one kind or another, there are few that offer the special excitement of an intensely experienced three-dimensional space.
It would be difficult to find more than a handful of projects with
open spaces possessing spatial characteristics noticeably above aver-

age. Most of recent development would be judged substandard compared with the work of earlier eras, despite the fact that there are many projects with self-contained spaces where total design control was vested in one designer. For some reason, positive space— one of the most powerful design qualities—is absent from much that has been built.

Have the value and importance of spatial definition been collectively forgotten, or have they simply been displaced by a burgeoning agenda of new design concerns? Recent architectural history has seen buildings that appear incredibly light and airy, buildings as gigantic abstract sculptural objects, buildings viewed as social development tools, and the exploration of the potential of new building products and technologies. Pursuit of such concepts might leave very little room for the oldfangled notion of spatial definition. Alternately, the idea of spatial definition may have been deliberately set aside during the modernist design revolution when traditional architectural values were under concerted attack. In the search for the primitive roots of art, artists turned away from the idea of rendering three-dimensional relationships, a shift of emphasis that no doubt profoundly affected the parallel development of modern architectural principles. Whatever the cause, the result has been the eradication from today's architectural language of both the importance of enhancing space and the means of achieving it.

Consider the following scenario: At a predesign conference with architects, an urban designer emphasizes the importance of reinforcing street scale and space, pointing out how the existing buildings in spite of their individuality manage to work together to give the street a special sense of space and place. The architects nod their heads and make a few pertinent remarks regarding the way the existing buildings interact to demonstrate their awareness and then go forth to design. Returning to present their effort, drawings are pinned on walls, models set up, the pocket pointer extended, and the presentation patter begins. The architect begins with how the building form evolved, moves on to the utter refinement and sophistication of alternate curtain wall studies, and then boldly addresses the street space and scale issue with, "and we continue the line of the adjacent cornice with an incised line here." At that point the urban designer realizes with dismay that while the architect may have understood the intent of his comments he did not know how to go about reinforcing street scale and space.

Understanding Spacial Perceptions

Explaining the cause of the urban designer's dismay requires a short technical detour. A fundamental fact is that in a very real sense, man's normal posture of looking at the world is the audience to which buildings and street frontages must play. On the stage of this theater, there are zones where features can be seen with great clarity and zones where only bold and sharply delineated forms will be perceived. In designing urban places for the human eye, it must occasionally be remembered that people see much more than they think they see, and they think they see everything in much greater detail than in truth they do.

The way people see and how the human eye works plays a key role in how people experience the world around them. During most of their waking hours people are conscious mainly of those things in the center of their vision on which their eyes are focused. Awareness of the role of peripheral vision surfaces only when it alerts people to a movement or potentially dangerous situation outside of their zone of attention. The extent of peripheral vision can be easily explored when someone looks at a point straight ahead and moves his hands in a arc from that point to the outer edges of his vision. It may come as a surprise just how far back he can see his hands before they disappear from view. In a horizontal plane most people can see sightly better than 180 degrees without moving their eyes, and in a vertical plane vision encompasses approximately 130 degrees, with eyebrows limiting vision upward about 20 degrees more than down.

If someone arranges himself before a mirror is such a way that he can see his fingers to one side at the very edge of his peripheral vision and also see the same fingers in the mirror near the center of his vision, he can compare the marked differences in quality between the two images. The mirror vision of his fingers is sharp and clear, but the view out of the corner of his eye is both blurred and lacking in color rendition. The differences occur because of the distribution of receptors in the eye's retina. The receptors near the visual axis in the center of the eye are densely packed and enable minute differentations to be observed, while toward the edges they are widely spaced and yield only crude impressions. However rough and imperfect peripheral vision is, it plays a crucial role in perception of space and volume. Only peripheral vision possesses the range essential to grasp the sense of a large volume. A major problem with much current design is that it is conceived almost entirely for appreciation by the center eye with no regard for the limitations of the peripheral field of vision where subtleties tend to disappear.

It is well known that few people (except bureaucrats) walk around with their eyes fixed straight ahead. When people enter a strange new place, they automatically scan the parameters of the space, pausing only to study features of interest. The 180- by-130 degree field of vision enables people to quickly and efficiently synthesize an overall mental image, provided the setting is not too complicated. If the design features are too simple and bland, they may not brother with a more careful examination and depend on their peripheral vision and memory for an overview. In such a situation people are apt, out of boredom, to shift their mental gears to other matters. People enjoy reexamining familiar areas where multiple levels of visual enjoyment are offered and where there always seem to be new visual relationships and effects to appreciate. If a building or group of buildings is to work on a day-to-day basis, a certain simplicity and boldness of feature and form is needed to facilitate comprehension of the larger composition and a degree of complexity and subtlety also is needed to renew the interest of the regular viewer. In recent years there has been more inclination toward the opposite, with the creation of a confused, disorganized overall composition in public spaces and provision of a poverty of visually interesting detail to sustain the day-to-day visitor.

How proposed projects are studied is quite different from the way built projects are typically experienced. To an excessive degree, proposed designs are evaluated through photographs and small models. The nature of human vision makes it difficult to evaluate the reality of a project via any kind of photographic process or small-scale model. Both techniques collapse everything down within the scope of the most perceptive part of the retina where features that will almost completely vanish in real life seem to play a significant role. Designers must recognize that to be effective many features must be overscaled or otherwise reinforced so that they will not wash out and disappear on the full-sized building.

Unlike a room, a plaza has no ceiling to define the height of the space within its walls and unlike a plaza a street has only two walls with which to define space. If those walls are low in relation to the width of the street, views outward are not contained enough to provide a sense of unifying space. The range of human vision thus affects the perception of street space and scale.

Designing for Vision

STREET SPACE

1:4 Ratio

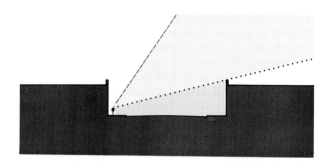

Height-to-Width Ratios

In a street with a 1:4 ratio of street wall height to width, there is three times as much sky as wall within the normal range of vision. The weak sense of space that streets of such proportions obtain has its counterpart in the very low and wide rooms popular in modern convention hotels. A typical modern "Grand Ballroom" may have floor dimensions of 80-by-125-feet and a ceiling height of 20 feet or less. A common observation about such spaces is that in spite of the large horizontal dimensions the visitor tends to experience the space as a sequence of smaller spaces, subdivided by tables, chairs, and people. In a street with a cross section of this proportion, the most noticeable sense of spatial definition occurs along the sides of the street where buildings, awnings, signs, and the curb line may combine to define a narrow band of space. Good spatial definition may not be impossible in a 1:4 proportioned street section, but it is extremely difficult to accomplish.

When the ratio is decreased to 1:2 the peripheral glimpses of sky equal the amount of visual field devoted to the street wall. The sky view is less important, however, in that it is in the less perceptive peripheral zone. The 1:2 ratio provides sufficient spatial containment to permit the creation of intensely three-dimensional space. A room with a similar cross section also would not appear oppressively low nor would the resulting space tend to fragment into subareas as in

1:2 Ratio

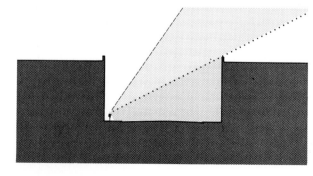

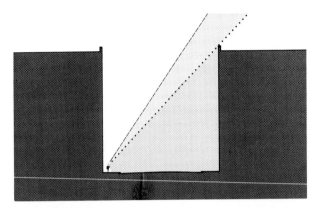

1:1 Ratio

the modern "Grand Ballroom" example. A 1:2 ratio is the minimum desirable ratio of height to width for good street spatial definition.

A street wall height that equals the street width will severely limit any skyview. The viewer can wholly comprehend the height of surrounding buildings with his peripheral vision although his vision is almost completely contained. Strong spatial definition is possible within such a cross section.

When the street wall height to width ratio is increased to 3:2, the top of the building is no longer visible without adjusting the angle of the head, and when the ratio is higher still it starts to become difficult to judge height because of the extreme angle. Higher street walls also increasingly restrict the amount of sunlight available to illuminate and help define the space, although when sunlight does penetrate the effect may be far more dramatic due to the increased contrast in light values. Extended areas enclosed by very tall buildings may seem claustrophobic to some.

The height at which the building cuts off peripheral vision is very near the angle of the Golden Mean.

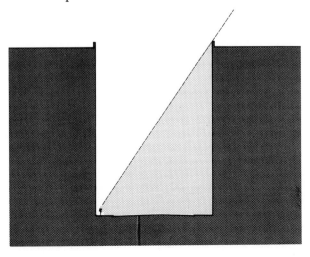

People do not stand in one place and stare fixedly across streets as represented in the previous diagrams; their restless natures usually compel them to walk down one street or another. Unless lost in some reverie, it is normal for people to look about a bit as they walk down a street and they are more likely to look along the street than across it. The angles of vision illustrating the street cross sections provide only a crude approximation of the predominate pattern of observation, but they do offer insight about how buildings and the spaces defined by them are perceived.

Assessing Scale

Obtaining the right street wall height to width ratio is the essential first step in defining street space. If the height is inadequate, good spatial definition becomes extremely difficult if not impossible to achieve. When street wall height effectively contains the channel of space, the next step is providing the means for the viewer to assess the dimensions of the space in terms of height and length—a hierarchy of scaled features must be established both vertically and horizontally. Further, it must be expressed in three dimensions or it will not work because any two-dimensional design tends to be subservient to the planar quality of its surface. The hierarchy must provide the means for reading the building height in easy, comprehensible terms, i.e., the reference scale for judging the larger whole should be of a size with which most people are familiar. At the larger end of the hierarchy, the scale element may be similar to a two-story commercial building, a common enough feature of the American cityscape. At the smallest end of the scale, people-sized elements provide useful reference points.

Overcoming Handicaps

Most streets have neither roofs nor ends and are often framed by buildings of disparate size, conditions which pose special design problems in the definition of street space and scale. To overcome these handicaps two design conditions must be met: (1) irrespective of the height of buildings, a relatively uniform height of street space must be defined to give the street cross section the strong unifying proportions of a well composed room; and (2) the facades framing the street should provide such grips, holds, and snags upon the street space as to fix it in place, offsetting the linear thrust of the street channel.

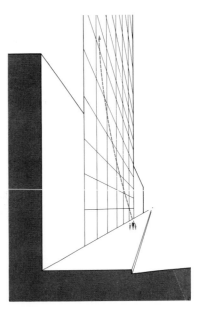

This facade defines a geometric plane that extends from the sidewalk to the top of the building. Windows and arcades are cut into the facade, but nothing projects beyond or intercepts the thrust of the vertical plane.

High-Rise Issues

It has been noted that where the buildings fronting a street are too low, it becomes impossible to suggest an appropriate ceiling to the street space. But if not designed thoughtfully, very high buildings that exceed the range of our peripheral vision also make defining the street ceiling height difficult. The reasons are quite different. Recent fashions in high-rise design have dictated building skins that proceed from the top to the ground in a single unbroken sweep. There may be indentations, but the outer plane always remains sacred and inviolate. The eye all too easily slides up a plane to infinity, and the absence of any firm stopping points leaves the pedestrian with no visual support for the perception of a human-scaled street space. This is not to say that in its crisp perfection, a vast pure geometric plane that suggests an infinitely larger plane extending into

62

space is not a marvelous intellectual notion that can also be satisfying theater. But it must be in the right setting, and in many situations it is a potentially destructive idea that should not be used without regard for its effect on the spatial environment of people. A vast geometric plane might be acceptable as a unique exception to the general urban fabric, but multiplied many times the aggregate effect can become alienating.

Building Bases
Compounding the scale problems that result from the virginal unbroken plane is the difficulty modern architects seem to have bringing tall buildings down to the ground. The bases of high-rise buildings rarely reflect the scale of the building. Standing near many high rises, you cannot tell from the architecture whether they are nine or 90 floors in height. For some unknown reason the architects of some of the tallest buildings in the world have elected to use base designs so low and horizontal they would be at home in a suburban

Neither scale has numbers on it, but one would be much easier to use than the other.

The horizontal striped pattern on this building is similar to the scale without inch and half-inch marks. It is difficult to judge its scale.

shopping mall. The gigantic Sears Tower in Chicago, for example, rests on a one-story base that looks like a misplaced furniture store from the Chicago hinterland. It does nothing for the street or the space around it.

Indentations, incised channels, or grooves do not interrupt the geometric plane or stop the eye from sliding up the surface. Indentations appear little more than a surface pattern on the plane.

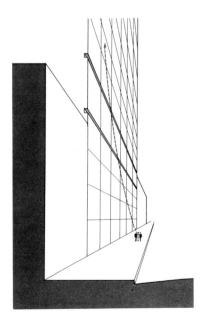

Effective Definition

The extended architectural plane remains a problem even if given a pattern. A window module endlessly repeated, or an all-vertical or all- horizontal striped pattern, will not offset the tyranny of the plane or provide a useful scale for appreciating the dimension of space. It is as if someone were given a scale or ruler where only the smallest increment of measurement was provided and there were no differing lines to distinguish one-eighth, one-half and one inch units of measurement. Such a scale would be useless for measuring anything thicker than a thumb.

Thus, to effectively define the height of street space it is necessary to interrupt the vertical thrust of the tall building, and to forcefully conclude facades at a height appropriate to the creation of a gracious street space. The strength with which the street ceiling or roof line requires definition depends on the degree of reinforcement provided by nearby buildings. The more reinforcement, the greater the design latitude. While there is no absolute rule for determining the best height at which to establish street space, the

64

A projection stops the upward slide of the eye. If made strong enough, the shadow line of a projection will register in the peripheral vision even if the viewer is focusing on pedestrian-level activities.

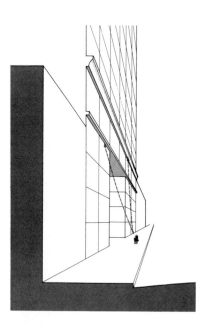

The newer buildings on the left side of the street fail to respect what had been so carefully achieved on the right. The call to symmetricality by the axial placement of the Chicago Board of Trade Building is ignored. In not picking up and reinforcing the pattern of belt courses, the spatial definition of the street is weakened.

The Mills Building in San Francisco was one of the few downtown survivors of the earthquake and fire. Postquake builders carefully coordinated the belt courses of major projects, extending variations on the lines of the Mills Building in several directions. The architect of the bland new building did not get the message and the street lost some of its unity.

The bold sculpturing of this building base contributes to the rich definition of street space and scale. The belt courses are perfectly aligned with those of the Mills Building.

66

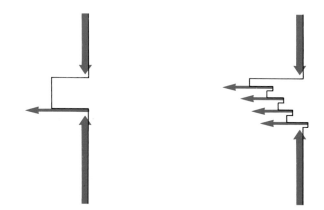

Both projections will interrupt the facade plane, but the projection on the right generates a much stronger sense of geometric planes extending into space.

street sections presented earlier demonstrated that a minimum height of one-half the width of the street is desirable to maintain a well-proportioned space. A maximum height of 1.4, multiplied by street width, is dictated by the outer limits of our peripheral vision.

Scale Defining Devices

Belt courses, cornices, and other design devices work to help define street space and scale in urban areas where enough traditionally designed buildings remain to establish a coherent pattern. The designers usually did not rigidly line them up except in formal compositions such as a civic center where common alignment was important to the overall concept. Instead, they often played interesting and curious design games, reversing emphasis, introducing additional lines, or pursuing a careful stepping up and down over the distance of several buildings. The underlying working design principle is simple and easily adapted to a variety of design languages and styles. The objective is to interrupt the upward rise of tall buildings in a way that suggests the presence of a horizontal plane extended into space. A single building so treated may have little effect, but when several such buildings are grouped together the effect is compounded, defining by inference a roof over the street.

Longitudinal Dimensions

Defining the longitudinal dimensions of the space on long straight streets is as critical as defining height and width. Even on streets where curves or hills prevent the contained space from leaking out toward an infinite horizon, the provision of horizontal scale should not be neglected. Streets lined by varied, relatively narrow facades that generate a definite if irregular rhythm have a built-in measur-

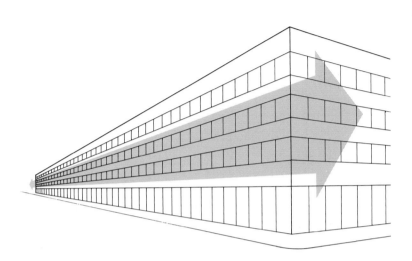

No useful scale for measuring distance.

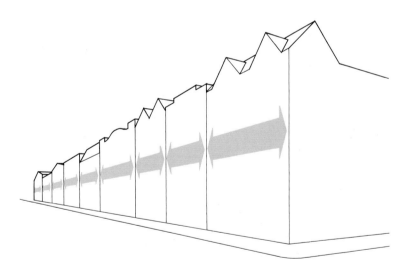

A built-in unit of measure.

ing device for appraising the longitudinal dimensions of street space. Where the buildings fronting a street are long and extended, or otherwise so bland as to appear homogeneous, the effective unit of measure may be so large to be useless as a measure of space.

68

Smooth, slick polished walls do not grip or hold space well. In sloping away from the street, the building further disengages itself from the task of defining space. The building seeks to become a special object in space at the expense of street space.

The deep-set windows and rusticated stonework of this facade grip and hold space well. It is not necessary to design in this style to apply the design principles involved.

Space has a quicksilver nature that makes it an elusive quarry to capture and define. If the cage is not tight enough, it quickly seeps out and dissipates. Holding space in place requires not only strong walls but walls that grip and hold slivers and chunks of space. This is accomplished by deep, large-scale indentations, bold sculptural projections, and a rich texture.

We can find basic space-defining principles imbedded in the masonry walls that frame so many of the world's great spaces. Masonry construction imposes a stringent order on the builder: the higher the building, the thicker the supporting walls needed and the larger the span the greater the effort required. The force of gravity is apparent throughout. Weight is unambiguously carried down to the ground, and the uppermost brick is joined to the ground by the visible structural response to the demands of gravity. The building's weight and mass are delineated by the joinery's intricate pattern and the subtle effect of minute differences in the alignment of the parts.

Light and airy buildings, ultraflat smooth facades, and polished reflective surfaces are opposite in character to the masonry wall and do not define space well. Decoration, long considered a useless activity and waste of material, now can be viewed in light of the requirements for spatial definition. Decoration has a function to the degree that it helps hold and define space, and it can be used, for example, to offset the light- reflective surface of a glass curtain wall and produce a building that works well with its more traditional neighbors to define street space.

CAPTURING, DEFINING SPACE

A taut reflective glass facade provides interesting optical effects but has no value for defining space or imparting a sense of scale. The inability to see into the building and sense the activity within creates an alien inhospitable setting. Such facades are at their best surrounded by lush landscaping or rising from a tight cluster of contrasting buildings.

Defining space can be done with smooth, thin-skinned buildings only by performing exceptional architectural acrobatics. In raising the mass of this office building into the air, a large volume of space was created then defined by the horizontal underside of the tower.

At the turn of the century, decoration had become an end in itself for many architects. The modernist revolution, with considerable justification, threw out this approach. But unfortunately, the revolutionaries elected the opposite extreme; affecting a bare undecorated look and overlooking the functional role of decoration in defining and enriching the quality of space.

PLAZA SPACE

Plazas are first and foremost urban spaces. They differ from parks and squares in that the emphasis is on creating a volume of space by architectural means—trees and landscaping generally play a small or nonexistent role in plaza design. Plazas come in many shapes and sizes and serve many purposes. They can be quiet dig-

The gymnastics this building performs have an evident effect on the character of surrounding space. However, the space lacks a central focus; no clearly defined place is created by the effort.

nified places to sit in the sun and enjoy a leisurely cup of coffee. They may be designed to dazzle people with a moment's grandeur at the entrance to an important sector of the city or to provide room for the daily crush of people to sort out their individual destinations. Busy or calm, functional or symbolic in nature, there is one thing a plaza should never be: an urban nonevent. Yet, all too many of the so-called plazas built during the past 15 years are just that. Instead of contributing to the enrichment of the city, unsuccessful plazas add to its fragmentation and dilution and rather than enlarging the opportunities for public enjoyment they merely consume space. There is nothing innately good about a plaza. Creating a successful plaza space requires a special set of conditions and if those conditions cannot be met, an alternate design objective should be considered.

Plazas built within the tight confines of a medieval street pattern benefit from the strong spatial containment and drama that accompanies a sunny open space that is reached only by narrow and deeply shaded streets. The visitor does not gradually proceed into such a space; he enters it in one step as he would enter a room. Because the space is an exception to the general pattern of tight narrow streets, it acquires special significance. Few places in urban America afford the opportunity to create dramatic entry sequences as do the narrow streets of ancient cities. More often the plaza will be entered from one or more wide streets. Additionally, if the surrounding buildings are office towers of recent vintage, they are unlikely to contain and define the street space because of the miscellaneous setbacks common to such buildings which erode potential contrast between plaza and street. These design problems should be dealt with in the decision to create a plaza.

Modern streets are most often open-ended linear arrangements and when street space is defined it remains part of a continuum. Plazas, on the other hand, are discrete spatial entities that focus inward. Plaza space should have the feel of an outdoor room and possess an intense three-dimensional quality.

Spatial Quality Factors

The quality of spatial containment is controlled by seven interrelated factors: size, shape, continuity, height of frame, floor configuration, architectural characteristics of the surrounding buildings, and sculpture.

After years of letting suburban-styled development erode its urban character, San Diego opted for an injection of instant urbanity. Instead of a typical bland shopping mall, Horton Plaza promises a complex sequence of spaces and pedestrian walkways reminiscent of medieval Perugia.

"The design of the center started as a typical suburban shopping center dropped into the heart of downtown, walled and fortified to protect it from the dangers of its urban setting. Outcries from the local design professionals and political bodies led to a change of architects and subsequently the design which has continued to evolve."—Michael Stepner, assistant planning director

Size

The larger the plaza, the more difficult it becomes to create an intense three-dimensional effect. Thoughtful observers have suggested a maximum size of approximately 200-by- 500 feet. Beyond these dimensions space begins to overwhelm the individual and spatial definition is very difficult to attain. These dimensions were arrived at from observation of important European plazas created in earlier eras when architecture was more cohesive and decision making was centered in a few skilled hands. The poor space-defining qualities of much contemporary architecture and development suggest that wisdom may lie in more modest objectives, say 200-by-275 feet. The optimum size of a plaza is also linked to the height of the sur-

The size of a plaza is the size of the space, not just the area of fancy paving. To think of the space as not including the abutting streets is to invite error.

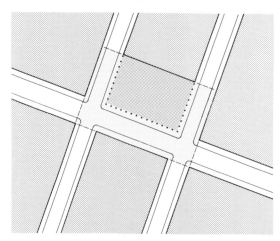

rounding framing buildings; generally the width should not exceed height by a factor of 3:1, however under certain conditions this may be pushed to 4:1 and still work.

Case Study: Boston Government Center Plaza. The plaza around Boston City Hall represents the first major American effort to create the modern equivalent of an Italian Renaissance plaza. The centerpiece Boston City Hall, by Kallmann, McKinnell and Knowles, is prototypical of a good space-defining building. It demonstrates that modern styling is no impediment to the objective of defining space. Regrettably the concept fails to come off successfully in spite of the excellence of the city hall design. The size of the space created around the city hall is the chief culprit.

The plaza is large enough to engulf both piazzas San Marco and Del Campo on the Cambridge Street side and unless there is more infill, they could also be repeated on the east side. Perhaps it was thought that somehow the street space was not part of the plaza space, or that the inward pressing curve of the great arching Center Plaza Building (c) on the west side of Cambridge Street would compensate for the excessive size of the space, but even the city hall's massive form (a) is not enough for the vastness of the space. The

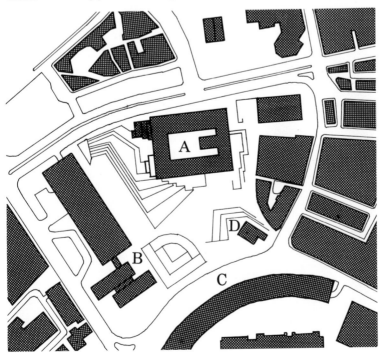

The piazzas San Marco of Venice and del Campo of Sienna can almost be fitted twice into the open space around Boston City Hall.

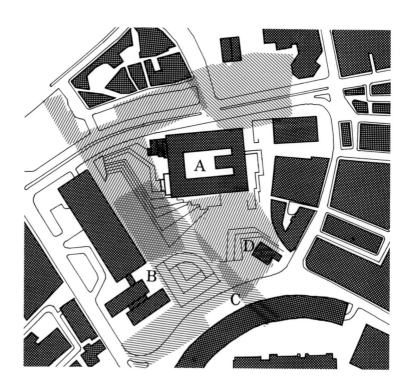

Adding perimeter buildings around the plaza would bring the area down to spatially workable dimensions.

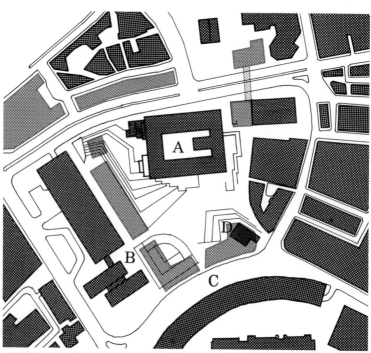

unfortunate configuration and character of the J.F.K. Federal Office Buildings (b) with their own little suburban plaza spaces, and the small bump of the "T" System stop (d) that is neither a building nor a nonbuilding, contribute in their own ways to weakening the already overextended space. The sunken fountain area in the northwest corner offers pleasant relief to the uncomfortably large plaza space but does nothing for the space.

The problem at least has the virtue of being correctable if the citizens of Boston retain the initial vision and follow through at some future propitious time. There is sufficient room for another building or linear concatenation of buildings to fit around the edge of the plaza to reduce its size to more amenable dimensions. Simultaneously, the new plaza frame would provide a needed covered walkway for inclement or sultry weather. A truly exciting space could be achieved with careful attention to the architectural nature of the new frame and other adjustments to close the gap on the north side of the city hall.

Height of Frame

The buildings composing the frame generally should be of a uniform height that does not vary more than 25 percent. The more uniform the frame, the easier it becomes to suggest the presence of an invisible ceiling to define the height of the space. While there is no maximum height prescription, allowing for a generous amount of sunlight to the plaza surface is essential for human use and enjoyment. Very large towers can overwhelm a small-scale frame that is not high or visually strong.

The uneven height of buildings framing the square yields a poorly contained space. The cluster of low buildings on the right side permits otherwise contained space to "leak" out.

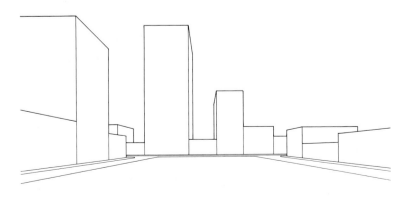

Under certain conditions the 1:2 height to width ratio needed to effectively define street space may be stretched to a 1:4 ratio in the design of plazas. This can be done when the frame is exceptionally uniform in height with only narrow interruptions. An adjacent tower element is needed to serve as a kind of spatial tent pole to offset what otherwise might appear as low and wide proportions.

Shape

The shape of a plaza should permit the space to be experienced, in its entirety, from any point within. Simplicity of form—one that can be easily comprehended—is also a desirable quality. People's impres-

The nearly uniform height coupled with a 1:3 ratio of building height to width give strong definition to the enclosed space of the plaza.

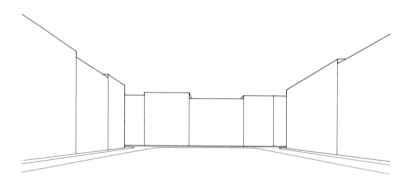

A tall tower that is almost as high as the plaza is wide facilitates the containment of space by a frame as low as 1:4. The tower functions as the main tent pole to the space increasing the average height-to-width ratio.

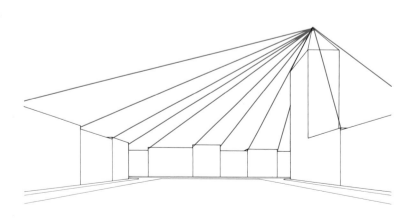

sion of the whole depends in part on the mind's ability to complete the forward picture with an image of what they know to be behind their backs. A form that facilitates the easy assembly of a total impression, such as a simple easily recognizable shape, is most effective in this regard.

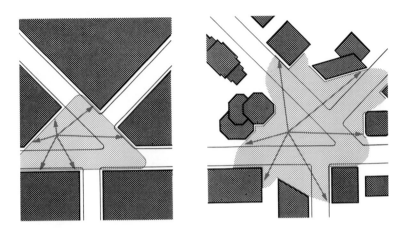

Left: A simple, easy to comprehend space.

Right: An amorphous, complicated, and ill-defined space.

The alignment of the defining walls can help compensate for critical gaps in containment. Concave curving walls that wrap around and cradle a central volume are particularly effective at containing space; their use could help offset the deficiency in a plaza that cannot avoid a serious gap in the plaza frame. Michaelangelo solved the problem of the missing fourth wall (a) of the Campidoglio by canting the flanking sidewalls inward (b) at the mouth of the opening to give the plaza form a positive grip on the space. Skewing opposed walls at angles to each other (c) can initiate dynamic tension between them that also helps compensate for other problems.

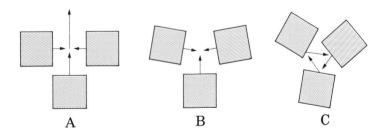

A   B   C

Floor Configuration

Where the individual buildings are strong and their design inter-action is paramount, then a flat plaza floor that offers minimum impedance is desirable. If, on the other hand, the buildings suffer from a degree of discord or there is a serious breach in the frame, then the careful sculpturing of the plaza floor can be used to counterbalance the deficiencies. Dropping the plaza floor down a few steps from the building plane introduces a powerful set of lines circum-

The crescent is among the most effective of space-defining forms, capturing space within the embrace of its curve.

The concave side of the Center Plaza Building, away from Boston City Hall, much more effectively contains space than the convex side facing the larger plaza.

scribing the central space and provides an extra set of defining lines. Sculpturing the floor to create a bowllike form turns the floor into a space container that reinforces the action of the walls. In doing this it is important not to divorce the sculptured portion of the floor from the perimeter. There must be a continuum on all sides. When a section of the plaza is simply dropped down without transition, the spatial proportions of the sunken part are determined by its walls, not the buildings framing the space above. On the upper level the sunken plaza often has a deleterious effect on the clarity of the space.

Case Study: Piazza del Campo. Of all the plazas in Italy, the Piazza del Campo generates the richest, most stunning sense of space. The remarkable thing is that the buildings framing the plaza, except for the gothic Palazzo Publico, are fairly straightforward masonry buildings, lacking the deeply carved features that help define space. Pride being what it was in Renaissance Italy, this may not have been of choice but of economic necessity. Whatever the reasons, the Sienese came up with a brilliant solution that did not require dazzling architecture to create a vibrant space. Instead of attempting to build the typical level plaza, they used their hillside location to advantage by creating a vast reservoir of space held in place by the strong wall of the Palazzo. The embracing curve of the uphill wall and the shallow bowl carved in the floor are the primary sources of this plaza's powerful sense of space. It is a remarkable

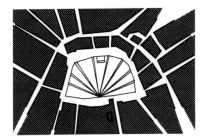

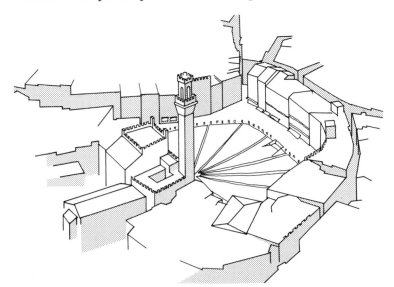

demonstration of how plaza shape and floor configuration can help offset the limited space-defining capacity of the buildings.

Continuity

Clarity of form and closure are weakened when continuity of the plaza frame is broken by wide roadways or other openings. The streets that breach the frame also invade the floor of the plaza, and if the traffic is heavy it will disturb the perception of the frame, subdividing the space with a moving partition of vehicles. Any roadway entering the frame becomes a part of the plaza space, and to think of the plaza as somehow separate from the roadway will yield a muddy concept and cause design errors. The number and size of openings that can be tolerated in the plaza frame is contingent on the strength and unity of the architecture. In some circumstances dense, large-scale landscaping can help close wide openings to more manageable proportions.

Case Study: United Nations Plaza.   With the construction of the Bay Area Rapid Transit system, a major plaza was called for at the point where the main axis of San Francisco's Beaux Arts civic center met the major commercial spine of the city. A plaza at this location could never be a tightly defined space, as Market Street was 120 feet wide and the intersecting civic center axis (Fulton Street) was 140 feet wide. The only realistic choice was to direct efforts toward the creation of a "formal place"—something short of a true plaza. A powerful monumental sculpture was needed to overcome the fragmented nature of the frame and provide a central focus. It had to be tall enough to assert itself as the central element of the space and be near but not on the central axis of the civic center so that it would be visible from city hall but still permit processions to proceed on axis. A remnant sculpture of the preearthquake city hall,

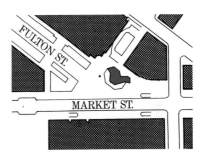

United Nations Plaza,
San Francisco

A photomontage shows how a nearby sculpture group, called the Pioneer Monument, would look in the plaza as compared to the existing black obelisk. With the monument in place, the clutter of poles becomes more noticeable.

Photographs by Hartmut Gerdes, Square One Film + Video.

now located at the wrong end of a one-way street, fit the spatial requirements and the character of the civic center very well, but the project architects rejected it in favor of designing a modern fountain of a sculptural nature. As built, the fountain consisted of large irregular blocks of granite carefully yet seemingly randomly arranged around the fountain basin. People are invited to climb and sit on the many levels to enjoy the water effects. The bulk of the granite blocks are built toward the outer edge of the plaza, with only a single irregular obelisk of polished black granite gloomily marking the spot where something taller and more grand should stand. The fountain is capable of many special water effects—or would be if the automatic controls were turned on. Unfortunately, it does not do what was needed: It does not address the plaza's spatial problems or provide a central focus for the plaza; its irregular form detracts from the clarity of the space; and its character is not sympathetic to the Beaux Arts architecture of the civic center.

Architectural Characteristics

The qualities of architecture needed to define space within a plaza are similar to those needed to define street space and need not be repeated here. There are, however, additional requirements stemming from the larger size of space being defined. The objective might be described as creating a three-dimensional graph by which the visitor can reference his movement across the plaza and comprehend the volume of the space. The most important lines of this graph are not upon the pavement but in the air, and are the implicit lines and planes projected into space by the surrounding buildings. Increments of height may be indicated by boldly drawn belt courses circumscribing the space at different levels. The axis lines projected by deeply recessed doorways and windows serve to subdivide the space into sectors. Out of the corner of the eye people are aware when they reach the centerline of a formally conceived facade and when they pass to the other side. The vertical plane defined by the juncture between abutting buildings also provides a measure of space and distance. The aggregate effect of many such features is the means by which people "read" space. Lines marked on the pavement can help reinforce the axis lines of the architecture, but cannot do the job alone for the simple reason that the pedestrian angle of view of the pavement becomes so extremely oblique that any patterning becomes quickly indecipherable.

Modern architecture turned away from the formally composed

The courtyard of H.H. Richardson's Allegheny County Courthouse is an exceptionally clear and lucid space that is defined by powerful architecture.

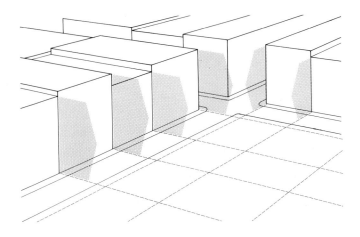

Vertical divisions between the facades of a row of buildings provide a scale with which to measure the space. This applies to streets as well as to plazas.

design to the formality of mechanical repetition. When the emphasis is dispersed over many small modules, the power of axis lines to subdivide space is drastically weakened. The shift toward two-dimensional facade designs also reduces the ability to accurately determine the alignment of an axis. When plazas are created in conjunction with a building, then the design of the building must address the spatial definition problems of the plaza. When a plaza is proposed, the ability of all the facing buildings to define space must be considered.

Case Study: Saint Mark's Square.   In seeking a suitable symbol of Venice's growing power and wealth, the original Piazza San Marco was doubled in length to 570 feet, creating serious problems in spatial definition. A number of important changes had to be instituted to compensate for the expanded size: The image of Saint Mark's Basilica was strengthened by wrapping a new facade around it which increased its width and formed deeply recessed and sculpted archways to project a powerful visual axis that helps organize the plaza space. Great visual unity was required to counteract the entropic effect of the distances involved, and to this end a facade of uniform effect was wrapped around three sides of the plaza. The unity of the frame helps underscore the exceptional nature of the basilica. Disengaging the 324-foot-high campanile from the frame to which it was once an integral part strengthened the campanile's role as the tent pole for the space and improved the unity of the frame.

Unlike Siena, Venice solved its spatial problems by architectural means. Fortunately, it could afford to do so without compromise.

The visual axis established by the deep arched entry portals to the Basilica San Marco are important organizing elements for the visitor.

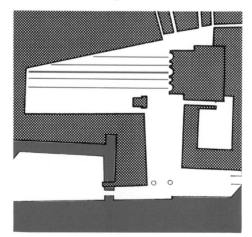

While the resultant plaza verges on being too large to provide a truly comfortable feeling, the brilliance of the composition is more than enough compensation.

Sculpture

Where the space-defining qualities of the framing buildings are weak or where wide roadways make containment difficult, the right use of large-scale sculpture can render victory from chaos. The great virtue of sculpture is its ability to capture and hold space and to provide a central organizing focus to a space. To do the job, the size and proportions of the sculpture must be appropriate to the space, and it needs to be positioned where it will generate the maximum tension in relation to its setting. The nature of the design problem must guide the selection of the sculpture: A low horizontal sculpture will have little effect on space except in its immediate vicinity, and solid monolithic forms do not grasp and hold space as well as more open forms. For most situations, a vertical composition through which space can move and flow and which captures some of that space within will be part of the prescription.

Case Study: The Chase Manhattan Bank Plaza. The Chase Manhattan Bank Plaza enjoys an exceptionally high degree of spatial containment compared with most American plaza building ventures. Entered from one of the narrow streets that approach it, the plaza appears as a definite surprise. When it was carved out of the dense Manhattan real estate, the plaza exposed building facades that were not designed to be seen in the way they are now presented and this deficiency was not helped by the way the raised part of the plaza podium acts to disengage opposite buildings from direct participation in the plaza.

In the 13 years before the Jean Dubuffet sculpture was installed, the Chase Manhattan Bank Plaza clearly lacked focus. The bank building placed its design energies into a soaring verticality and little into generating any spatially organizing forces. The sunken circular court with a sculptured floor by Isamu Noguchi had no effect on the larger volume. The sunken court may have appeared more significant on plans and when looking down at scale models, but its primary value is to let light into a lower level. The initial excitement of entering the space was quickly replaced by an anticlimactic reality: it was a dull, uninteresting space.

The installation in 1972 of Dubuffet's abstract sculpture of four

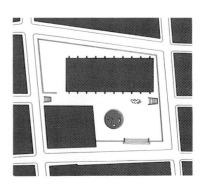

86

Photograph by Arthur Lavine.

trees fulfilled the original plans. The sculpture succeeded by itself
in changing the spirit and quality of the space to a remarkable degree. High and open, space moves through, in, and around the parts
of the sculpture. The nature of its form effectively captures and
holds the space around it, while its unique appearance provides an
arresting central focus to the plaza.

Case Study: Bank of America Plaza. The Bank of America Plaza
is located at the intersection of two streets which are several times
wider than those that lead into the Chase Manhattan Bank Plaza.
The plaza is on the north side of the 778- foot-high office tower,
which allows little sunlight to reach its surface. Strong winds frequently scour the plaza, so grandeur rather than amenity was perhaps the best that could be achieved. In its original form, the plaza
contained a sculpture and a low fountain that spilled water so carefully over its edges that it was difficult to tell if it was water or plas-
tic. The fountain has since suffered reincarnation as a kitsch garden
planter, but the sculpture, popularly dubbed "the banker's heart,"
remains intact. The black stone sculpture shows poorly before the
dark granite background on the sunless plaza floor, and the low solid

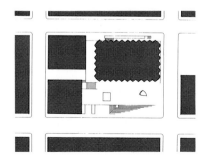

Space slides up, over, and around the sculpture but is not enhanced or activated by the sculpture's presence.

form of the sculpture does little to enhance the space about it. The end product is an essentially blank and poorly defined space that is little used or enjoyed. Installation of a large-scaled, light-colored sculpture of a nature that will hold and vitalize the space about it could recapture some of the windswept spaces around the base of the building for lively uses and attractions, and instill needed life into the space.

Flagpole Sculpture. Every now and then an attempt is made to use flagpoles as a sculptural element to enhance the spatial qualities of a plaza. Both the flagpole and the flag are visible from a distance, usually out of the plaza, and the splash of color can be delightful. In the plaza the flag is mostly out of sight and from its appearance the modern pole could be a utility pole. Looking down on a small model, the World's Fair Toothpick style flagpole gives the impression that it will contribute to spatial definition, but too often it tends to clutter vision rather than define space.

The equal realization of all seven factors that contribute to good spatial definition is an unlikely event. Fortune seems to conspire to demand a delicate balancing act, compensating for weakness in one area by developing extra strength in others. One of the designer's most difficult tasks is being able to step back and coldly examine weaknesses in the concepts that he has had a part in creating. Too often the excitement over the glory of the inner visions blinds him to the reality of what is actually proposed.

Applying the Factors

BEAUTIFICATION and RECREATION

Eloquent testimony for minimum landscaping standards.

Beautification is a popular but awful word that usefully describes actions aimed at making streets and neighborhoods more attractive and livable. It is an important activity made necessary by the way we build and live. In suburban areas, where landscaping and signage are often the dominant visual elements and the buildings tend to be little more than a symbol tucked behind a parking lot, beautification is supremely important. In such settings beautification becomes *suburban urban design*, a distinct subdiscipline with its own rules. As a general rule, the more urban the context, the more important architecture is, and the more suburban the setting, the more important beautification becomes.

Beautification efforts are likely to spring from several sources within a community: merchants unhappy over sagging retail sales, a neighborhood organization determined to get something done, or even a bored bureaucrat. This diversity of beginnings and purposes has the natural tendency to produce projects equally unrelated in effect. This may not cause serious design problems because the individual projects are usually benign, but the overall effect can needlessly suffer. The accumulation of unrelated improvements can reduce the value of the setting. When the individual features are attractive in themselves it becomes difficult to define the problem or find leverage for doing anything about it. It is best to avoid such situations by establishing simple and reasonable design guidelines for achieving the desired results (the easy part) and by consistently adhering to the guidelines over a long period of time (the hard part).

The design opportunities and problems inherent in planting trees along roadways offers a good example of these kinds of design guidelines. An arterial street differs from local streets in that it carries much more traffic that travels at higher speeds. It is a working, no-nonsense street used to travel longer distances and signals are often timed to facilitate the smooth flow of traffic. Arterial streets are most commonly landscaped with flanking rows of trees and, if space permits, a planted median. It is simple, straightforward, and matches the flow of traffic in a rather nice way. If all arterial streets in the community were landscaped in a similar way and other streets were treated differently, users would soon learn that any street so landscaped was an arterial roadway. When a person reached an unfamiliar intersection with such a street in anoth-

BEAUTIFICATION PROGRAMS

Traffic Definition

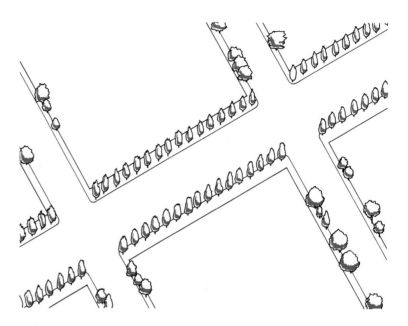

er part of town, he would recognize it as being an arterial street. Thus, beautification intended to make the roadway more attractive serves the additional purpose of helping to identify the arterial street system.

The random nature of beautification efforts is not exactly harmonious with such a disciplined approach. If many neighborhoods choose to landscape local streets in a manner similar to arterial streets, the system soon loses its special meaning. Maintaining the integrity of a system keyed by landscaping may require telling the block club whose heart is set on a double row of magnolias that it must use at least two different tree types and space the trees in irregular patterns to help differentiate the local street from arterials. Fortunately, very few people want their local residential street to be confused with an arterial street.

Landscaping also can be used to actively discourage through and fast traffic on residential streets. The most advanced designs for this purpose have been developed in England and Holland. (To be cute and knowledgeable at the same time, call them by their Dutch name of "Woonerf.") The psychology of the plans for Woonerven (plural) is that a straight line path coupled with a clear demarcation of auto and pedestrian paths encourages drivers to speed, and that removing those qualities will cause drivers to slow down. Working examples demonstrate that it works: The demarcation between ve-

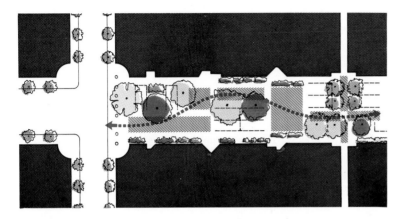

hicles and pedestrians is deliberately blurred. There are no continuous curbs, and the pavement is divided into several different patterns and textures. To proceed, the driver must follow an irregular path around parked vehicles, benches, and play areas. The appearance of the right-of-way is more that of a meandering private driveway than a typical street. The driver is made aware that he is sharing the same paved area with pedestrians. Everything about the design says that this is a street for people, and in the process the recreational value of the street space is enriched.

Ever since the Philadelphia Plan was adopted in the 1950s, a tree plan seems an essential part of an urban design study. The tree plan is a rather pretty document showing orderly rows of green dots (streets) linking larger clumps of green dots (parks). A few recognizable buildings are shown to help the viewer figure out what he is looking at. The great virtue of such a drawing is that it dramatically illustrates how important trees can be within the urban landscape.

There are many good reasons for making a tree plan. Dollar for dollar, trees are probably the best urban design investment a community can make. Further, people like trees, and not wholly irrelevant, a tree plan is good for at least 15 minutes' presentation time before a warmly responsive audience. However, what is too often forgotten over time is that the dramatic importance of the linking rows of trees is dependent upon the adjacent streets not having trees. When there are trees on every street, the symbolic linking street might be the street where trees are removed. An effective plan must state not only where and how to plant trees but also in-

Beautifying with Trees

dicate where trees should not be planted. When tree plantings are being used to distinguish certain streets or districts, a fairly high degree of contrast is needed if the difference is to be apparent to a casual observer who lacks a deep interest in fine botanical differentiations.

Here are some design guidelines that a community might apply to the planting of trees:

• On local streets where through and fast traffic is to be discouraged, tree planting should suggest an irregular stop and go character by the uneven spacing of clusters and dense constrictions of overhead foliage at intervals.

• Through streets, intended for longer trips, can be appropriately expressed by landscaping that maintains a constant character and a continuous even rhythm. The faster the traffic flow, the longer the length of the repeating module and the more open the street should be.

• Tree shape and height can be used to denote different kinds of streets. Slight differences in tree types are not likely to be recognized by most people; to be effective the differences must be sharp.

• Distinctive tree types and planting patterns can help provide a physical identity around which neighborhood organizations can crystalize when strong geographic boundaries are lacking.

• A shopping district on a through street can be identified by using a different tree type yet retaining the overall rhythm. If the primary tree was evergreen and the shopping district was lined with deciduous, the arrangement would ensure sun during the colder winter months and sharply define the district.

• In suburban areas where landscaping is so often the predominant visual element, trimmed trees can provide the strong forms needed to set off an important activity area.

There is no earthshaking breakthrough in the preceding ideas about tree planting. Cities and towns have consciously or unconsciously applied these or similar principles for decades if not for centuries. The guidelines are simple and work if followed. The same underlying approach can be applied to many other common pieces of urban hardware. Street lighting, bus stop shelters, benches, signing, awnings, and paving all can be directed toward accomplishing important community objectives beyond increasing the "niceness quotient" of an area. Similarly, the height, spacing, intensity, and color of street lighting can be directed to underscore the intended role of streets. A local shopping district can be made special by giving it a distinctive appearance through a unique signing program, the coordinated use of awnings, and/or the intensive use of brightly colored flowers.

Wherever beautification efforts are undertaken, the nature of the efforts should harmonize with the setting. The many individual actions should be coordinated to enhance the definition of residential districts and the community structure linking those districts. Strong neighborhood organizations are more likely to form where area boundaries are clearly defined. The design treatment of streets and shopping areas can help provide the needed framework where natural geographic boundaries are lacking. Articulating the system of local and arterial streets serves the same objective, and assists in making the physical organization of the city easier to understand. This is desirable for all citizens but is particularly critical for those such as the poor and uneducated who experience difficulty moving about the city.

Well-intentioned beautification efforts do not ensure that the result will be benign. Over the years, large and small urban design bloopers have been perpetrated across the American landscape and are uncomfortable reminders of the imperfection of our vision. It is healthy to remember exactly how easily enthusiasms of the mo-

Beautification Devices and Goals

Dense foliage masks much of these attractive buildings. Surrounded by lushly landscaped suburbs, the community might better have stressed rather than hidden its unique character.

ment can blind people to what really is being done. Where these momentary manias germinated—among the grass roots, the groves of academia, or the bureaucratic wasteland—is not so important as that while they flourished they completely skewed the vision of a great many people.

The Kiosk

There was a time that one could tell an urban designer was at work by the presence of a kiosk in a plan. At one moment in history kiosks, with their suggestive imagery of elegant posters by Henri de Toulouse-Lautrec and the urbane elegance of Paris, were almost synonymous with urban design. When they were installed upon the American street, the effect was something else. Where the Parisian model sported only a few well-spaced theatrical posters, the American version always managed to look like somebody's Kleenex collection: unreadable and unsightly. Somewhere there must be a kiosk that works, but the overwhelming evidence indicates that Americans lack the discipline to use them wisely. From time to time the ritual kiosks still appear on plans, but they are not so frequently or prominently displayed. A few fluttery fluffy kiosks do not make a design disaster, and who knows, in time we may learn how to use them.

The Flagpole

Next to the kiosk in popularity as a beautification device is the flagpole. Flags and especially long untangled banners are especially important features in renderings of urban design projects. The drawings usually present a viewpoint up among the pigeons and the flags and banners play a much greater role there than when seen from below. The real merits of the design can be better judged by trying to visualize the project without the banners. A related device that appears frequently is the circle of flagpoles, especially popular on gore corners. Why this particular design device gained currency is not clear, apparently it is thought of as an easy and relatively inexpensive way to occupy space and possibly achieve budget grandeur.

Flagpoles, unlike acceptable sculpture, can be ordered from a catalog. There are some limitations that should be considered in using flagpoles. First, the modern World's Fair Toothpick-style flagpole can only be experienced as such from a distance where the entire pole and flag can be seen. When standing close to such a pole it is difficult to distinguish from a utility pole. A flagpole should have a massive base that has its own presence and is not confused with clutter. When the monumental flagpole base was discarded as nonfunctional, its symbolic value was overlooked: It told everyone that it was an important pole bearing a proud emblem; it was not something the electric company put up to carry a few wires.

Prettiness

For the garden clubs of America, beautification means one thing: pretty, i.e., possessing the qualities of cuteness and charm. Prettiness is a perfectly valid design objective that is suitable for many situations, but like colored candy dessert topping it must be used with restraint. Few would enjoy having their salad, soup, and entree sprinkled with the same pink candy bits used on the birthday cake. But this is precisely what some communities set out to do. Consider an old sailing port, mining town, or historic settlement that is so decked out with hanging baskets of flowers, bright pastel colors, cute signs, and quaint displays that no matter how real the town under the surface is, it looks and feels more like a chunk of Disneyland. The sense of history—of older times, places, and ways—is a fragile commodity. It is found most easily lurking amid neglect and decay, and because it is so fragile we feel this should not be lost. Unfortunately, in the very zeal to preserve the objective is sometimes obliterated.

*Before: The Stanford Shopping
Mall in Palo Alto, California, before its recent architectural face
lift.*

*After: Architect John Field visually
narrowed the spaces between buildings and injected strong hard edge
architectural forms to contrast
with lush plantings and individual
storefronts.* Photograph by
Jeremiah Bragstad.

A little prettiness can go a long way. Even in the most syrupy television situation comedies the authors are careful to insert sharp cynical comments (referred to as treacle cutters) to provide some relief from the endless burbling chatter. The same principle is applicable to large projects and cities. For instance, as the competition between shopping centers increases there is evidence of a rapid escalation in the prettiness index. While this may be a decided improvement on the spartan shopping centers of past years, mass produced glitter can be stultifying. It is possible to take a reasonably dramatic space and so cute it up that any real excitement is smothered in visual clutter. The point is not to avoid prettiness so much as to make certain that when it is used it is balanced by a strong architectural or interior design treacle cutter.

Malls

Some of the most lushly illustrated examples of misguided improvements are to be found in the residue of mall mania that spread across the nation in the 1960s. Suffering from the middle class exodus to the suburbs and the competition from suburban shopping centers, downtowns were pleading for help. The urban doctors carefully examined the patient and prescribed injections of the very qualities that made the suburban competition so effective. Downtown shopping streets were to be turned into the urban equivalent of the suburban shopping mall. Fountains would sparkle in the sun and trees would arch gracefully over space where traffic once roared. The pedestrian streets of Europe so popular with vacationing intelligentsia would be recreated on American soil. Suddenly, American cities, so the Sunday supplement hype ran, were going to become as sophisticated and cosmopolitan as their European counterparts. At the time it seemed a reasonable hypothesis to an activist government interested in finding needs and filling them. Federal money went to work funding an interesting array of projects. As might be expected when something new is tried on a grand scale, some experiments worked and others did not. What seemed simple and straightforward was discovered to involve many delicate shadings. It is among the less sucessful examples that we can find the most clearly drawn lessons.

Urban Suburbanization

Inserting suburban features into an urban setting is a concept that is easy to express in words but is surprisingly difficult to resolve into a successful design. The differences between suburban and urban design are not superficial or easily masked. They start with the attitude of buildings toward the street and include building proportions, composition, materials, and the relationship to landscaping. While these differences are striking, many designers seem oblivious to the issues involved.

Transforming a city street into a mall is a response to the desire for a dramatic change that overtakes merchants when business is declining, but it is a direction loaded with difficult design problems. Unlike pedestrian streets created in the medieval sectors of European cities, American streets are much wider. The number of shoppers that would provide a lively bustle on a medieval street would appear lost and lonely on a wide American street. Unlike a narrow twisting street, a wide street cannot simply be paved with an attractive pattern; to avoid a desolate look the space must be filled so that a normal complement of shoppers will not appear forlorn. Overlooking the extreme differences between city streets and typical shopping malls, the designers packed the streets with the same kind of design devices used with success in suburban shopping malls.

Long, low, horizontal buildings frame the malls of suburban shopping centers, and the landscaping takes on a similar rambling character. Hexagonal planters of varying heights cluster together in an extended loose arrangement, interlocking pools of water zigzag across the space and low stepped terraces create a performance platform and informal seating, as well as sculptural composition. Suburban design rarely uses completely formal arrangements; when a formal axis is used it is usually played against informal cluster patterns to maintain a relaxed ambience.

Older city streets are quite different. Instead of long rambling buildings there are many narrow vertical buildings. Each is placed precisely on the property line and presents a formal face to the street. Where the suburban buildings maintain a casual stance, the urban buildings stand stiffly at attention, each trying to outdo the other in the splendor of its uniform. The two settings are so different that to take a design that works well in one context and insert it in the other is like wearing Bermuda shorts and flip-flops to a formal dance— it is asking for trouble. This is precisely what was attempted in many malls across the country.

"K" Street Mall, Sacramento.

Case Study: K Street Mall. Perhaps the most dramatic urban-suburban clash was achieved in the K Street Mall in Sacramento, California. Most of the buildings along K Street were built between 1890 and 1928, partly disguised by some facade modernization in the 1950s. Several buildings combine to form each block front. Each is well-mannered, respecting its neighbor and the street. For the most part they are vertical compositions, higher than wide, and painted and covered with a fair amount of decorative trim.

The design selected to beautify and transform the street could not have been more different in nature. Great sprawling abstract planes and massive wedges cast in monolithic concrete parade down the center of the street and form a visual and practical barrier for much of each block. Over these forms, water gushes and cascades in myriad ways. As modern art and as a water garden of sorts, the design possesses many attractive parts, but the concept could not have been more at odds with its setting. It might have fit in a shopping mall but on K Street it looked as comfortable as a beached whale. The design completely ignored the character of the street. It is clear that beautification efforts must be as careful of contextual relationships as buildings. In cases such as the K Street Mall it would seem that either the designer does not know what he is doing or he becomes so excited with the daring of a concept that he does not care.

RECREATION

A number of important studies done in recent years have significantly advanced our understanding of the qualities needed for popular well-used open space. The behavioral study work of William H. Whyte and others has verified the importance of seating, sunlight, wind protection, tables, food service, and visual amenities. The research provides important data in an area difficult to document.

It should be no surprise that when asked why they go some place, people will answer that it is because they like it. Questioning people about how they spend their free time tells us what they enjoy, but asking people hypothetically what they would like to do may illicit answers that have little in common with what they really would do if the opportunities existed. Their answers will also be limited to things with which they are familiar. These practical constraints make a realistic set of conclusions difficult to verify, leaving a great deal of room for interviewer bias.

People are a diverse lot. Some enjoy nothing better than gathering in a large noisy group; others look for a quiet corner to enjoy a good book. Younger people will sit on the grass in the hot sun while the older people may seek a dark cool bar because they have lost their tolerance for sunlight. Window shopping, browsing in a bookstore or library, visiting an art gallery or museum, watching a good tennis match, slipping into running gear for a five-mile jaunt, or arguing politics with friends are a few of the things people do or would like to do in their free time. They are things that make for a happier, healthier population and a more competitive city. Given the diversity of recreational activities demonstrated by people each day, it appears unwise to narrowly focus on a few kinds of facilities. Diversity should be encouraged even if some activities prove less attractive than others.

In dynamic downtown districts, interior recreational areas are easier to secure than is quality open space that is protected from wind and assured of reasonable sunlight. The areas around the elevator core on the ground and mezzanine levels of buildings present excellent opportunities for doing double duty. Expand the lobby space and provide the right kind of background surfaces and lighting and many lobbies would make lively places for either commercial or nonprofit art displays. Bring in a little sunlight and create a high airy space where people can sit to enjoy the art and an espresso and a special environment is achieved. Major corporations often seek to enhance their image through art displays in their lobbies but typically offer no place to sit, bad lighting, and the wrong background.

The pavement pattern must have looked attractive on the presentation boards. Unfortunately, winter storms whip across the Marine Midland Plaza, requiring the installation of handrails so people can get to the building. Solving the wind problem through design would have been much more to the point.

There are many activities that, when coupled with a well-run program and complementary commercial uses, can turn indoor space into lively yet suitable recreation zones. Compact sports such as handball, tennis, racquetball, shuffleboard, lawn bowling, and billiards attract audiences when competitions are organized between professional groups and businesses. Because of access problems, these uses will tend to be limited to projects with larger sites where they can be located at or near the ground.

Only the rare developer will voluntarily address the recreational needs of the workers in commercial buildings. Offering floor-area premiums for their inclusion or requiring their presence with the size based upon the total floor area and worker density can make providing such space attractive.

Exterior and interior recreational spaces should be integrated with beautification and urban design objectives. Recreational facilities can be made to serve large-scale urban design objectives without losing their recreational value just as beautification measures can be made to serve recreational needs without compromising the larger design objectives. Placing beautification, recreation, and formal urban design open space concerns into separate compartments results in an unnecessary waste of limited resources.

URBAN FORM and BUILDING FORM

Boxes on the Boston Skyline, 1983.

The external image a city presents to the world is the signature by which it is known. Like handwriting, a city's skyline conveys significant information about its nature. The pride with which the city's buildings assert themselves against the sky, the care with which buildings are set beside each other, and the response to the landform is evident in the views glimpsed when traveling toward a city. Beyond the pride and enjoyment of its citizens, there may be little practical use for a beautiful skyline except the attraction of visitors. Yet, there seem to be links between the outward appearance of a city and how it is experienced within and between a city that cares about its skyline and what that city becomes.

URBAN FORM DECISIONS

Only a few decades ago, decisions affecting the skyline rested in the hands of at least a few city residents. Civic concern regarding the skyline may not always have been uppermost but it was present. Today the shapes of new additions to the skyline often are determined by distant economic interests. Budgetary objectives almost exclusively dominate and civic concerns, if present at all, are pasted on as afterthoughts. This change in attitude is not invisible—it is imprinted forcefully upon the face of the city as new buildings displace old. But cities do not have to passively accept in the name of progress what the fates toss their way. Powerful tools are available to shape the height and form of individual buildings that, in aggregate, shape the city skyline.

Visibility

Traveling toward and through a city, what is seen and experienced is determined by the underlying landform, modified by the size, scale, and pattern of development. A flatland city can only be viewed as a whole if there is a large expanse of open land or water before the city. Once within the outer edge of development, even small buildings that line the streets, unless the streets are very wide, can screen much more substantial development from view. A city built on hills is seen quite differently. In the flatland city, only the upper parts of tall buildings are seen, primarily visible against the sky. In the hilly city, much more of a building's overall form is exposed and viewed against a backdrop of a large part of the city, or at least in context with a substantial part of the cityscape. Because of this tendency to look inward upon itself, residents of a hill-based city tend to evaluate a building quite differently than do citizens of its flatland opposite. One considers a building in the context of the other large buildings sharing the sky with it, the other adds its rela-

In flatland cities, small buildings in the foreground can block views of much larger buildings or divorce visible building tops from their immediate setting.

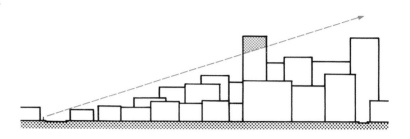

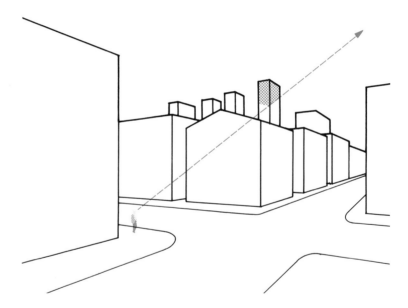

tionship to smaller buildings in the vicinity and incorporates the fine scale of a residential neighborhood that forms part of its background. A building that would appear a reasonable addition to one city could seem grossly overscaled in the other.

Form Relationships

The appropriate shape of buildings as they fit into and, in turn, shape the urban form is also influenced by topographic conditions. In a city of rolling hills where the aggregate form of buildings takes on the sensuous forms of the land, a building such as a large slab-shaped structure that generates strong horizontal lines will be seen as antithetical to the nature of the cityscape. Those same horizon-

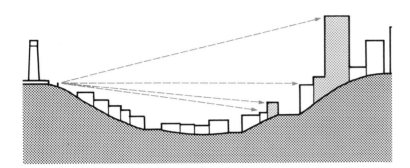

Within a hill-based city, large buildings may be entirely exposed to view within a context of much smaller buildings.

tal forms could be a desirable design objective in a flatland city. If the structure also blocks cherished views, esthetic concerns may be coupled with practical matters of dollars and cents. Views can have significant value in terms of rents and property values. Hills not only influence the kind of building forms that are desirable, they have impact on where tall buildings should or should not be placed. A large tall building built at the base of a hill not only will block views from the hill but also will detract from the hill's presence and form. The same building placed on top of the hill enhances the hill form and retains existing views.

A slab tower will block much more view than a similar sized tower with a square footprint.

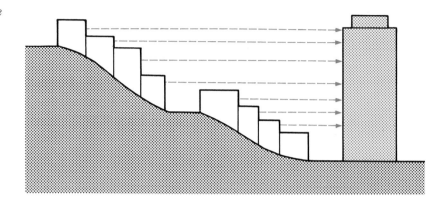

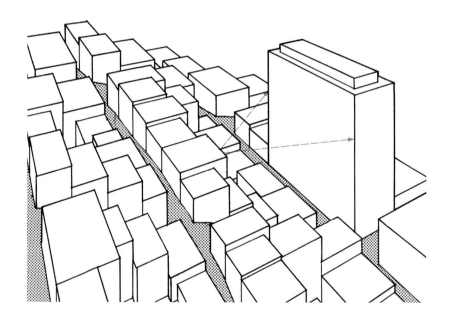

The construction of these towers and the threat of similar projects along the waterfront led to the adoption of citywide height limits in San Francisco.

Mountainsides and sharp breaks in topography of a grand natural scale appear capable of supporting a variety of urban design approaches. A looming mountainside is visually strong enough to sustain the contrast of a formally opposed design as well as a fine-scaled approach that follows the land.

Flatland cities have more developmental options than a similar scale of development in hilly terrain. The options range from the classic urban vision of the Emerald City to the creation of bold megaterraces of identically tall buildings. In the example illustrated, "benching," which is the lining up of building tops to define a horizontal plane, was deliberately sought to echo and dramatize the flatness of the underlying plain. In a hilly city such an approach would obliterate both the natural form of the land and block in-city views. Hills, by their limiting effect on traffic and because they are delightful to live on but make conducting business difficult, tend to assert their own order on a city. Flatland contains no such built-in directives, but the flexibility to evolve in many different ways can be a problem that requires the imposition of man-made order for its solution. Flatland Chicago meets Lake Michigan in a great urban escarpment, a man-made cliff fronting a fresh water sea. The effect is dramatic and satisfying. Chicago could have also stepped down to the lakefront for an equal if different effect. The land permits many approaches to the water's edge. In contrast, San Francisco's hills sweep gently down to the bay, dictating development to do the same or else disturb an established harmony. Where the underlying topography possesses strong characteristics it makes sense to work with and enhance that character wherever possible.

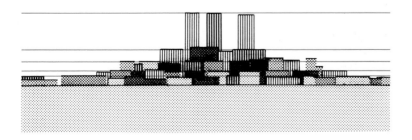

The more recent slab building, downhill on the right, violates the general pattern of development in this section of San Francisco.

CONTROLLING HEIGHT

Height limits are the primary but not the only means for controlling height. Sun access angles designed to assure direct sunlight to a park work in a similar way, differing mainly in their single-minded purpose and more evident sculpturing effect. Bulk controls governing the maximum horizontal dimensions and/or floor area also influence how high a developer will build, but are more uneven and unreliable in their effect, waxing and waning with changing market conditions. Density controls in and of themselves cannot be relied upon to limit height unless linked to maximum lot size or specific building types.

Height Controls

The need for height controls too often becomes apparent after irreparable damage has been done. San Francisco did not put its citywide height controls into effect until after a dozen or more towers and slabs were erected in incredibly sensitive areas and the city was threatened by larger, even more disturbing proposals. An urban design disaster may facilitate political action, but it does not result in the best plan. Height limits imposed after errors are made help ensure that more damage is not done but does not correct the damage. The misplaced tall tower often presents the urban designer with frustrating design dilemmas. A classic example is the 60-story John Hancock Building standing next to H.H. Richardson's Trini-

Height limits can be used in many ways to protect the architectural and symbolic integrity of important civil buildings.

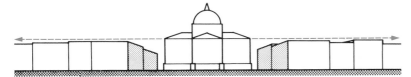

A. Dominance over all.

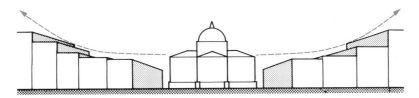

B. Dominance within a softly defined area.

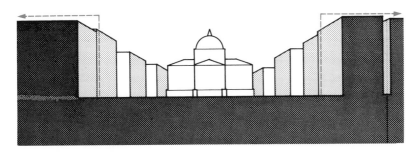

C. Dominance within a channel of space.

ty Church in Boston. The scale of the frame appropriate to the church and Copley Square appears to be in the vicinity of 80 to 100 feet, not the Hancock Building's 787 feet. The design question posed by this scale differential is this: Should the height for subsequent buildings be set to that of the ideal frame and the tower left to remain forever a single glaring exception, or should transitional height towers be built that will tie the Hancock Building into the cityscape but further dwarf Trinity Church? Before the John Hancock Building's construction, few would have dreamed such a tall tower would ever be built in that location. Now it is too late for anything but a compromised salvage job.

Studies have indicated that height controls are useful for distributing growth but are ineffectual in limiting growth except at the lowest height levels. Height limits will have a more certain effect at lower height levels because it is more likely development will engage them. Their impact is modified by land-use controls, the height selected, and the demand for floor space. In a booming "hot" office market, every project will attempt the maximum feasible construction height; in a weak economy, few projects may approach even moderate heights. That high towers can be built does not mean every developer will elect to do so; a special set of circumstances is required. Developers will build lower than the maximum height permitted when it is in their economic interest to do so. In the higher height districts, the actual physical results to be obtained from the imposition of height districts thus can be difficult to project over the short term as demand changes with economic cycles. They are more effective at limiting height from going above a specified elevation than achieving development at that height.

San Francisco's experience with the height districts established in 1971 illustrate the problems that can be encountered when developers choose not to build to the maximum in the highest height district. The adopted height plan permitted towers 700 feet high to be constructed in the heart of the financial district. It was hoped that at least one project would be built to that height to form the peak of a man-made hill of buildings and give needed balance to the dominating hulk of the Bank of America Building on the northern fringe of the core. The actual outcome was a row of towers all in the vicinity of 600 feet, with a resultant blunting of the skyline at that level. A few years later the nature of the high-rise market and architecture changed toward an increased emphasis on prestige qualities. Unfortunately, the change came too late for the key sites in the highest height district. The lesson is clear: Height limits are more effective at achieving sculptural form objectives within the typical height range of construction. To depend on the exceptional building to occur at the right place and time is to depend on luck.

The need for height limits is not limited to only rapidly growing high-density districts, as the random disposition of high rises in some low-density suburban areas shows. The visual effect of odd-shaped towers dotted across the landscape with no apparent or-

High-rise towers are beginning to pop up in scattered locations among low-rise suburban development.

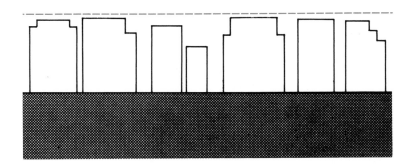

"Benching" occurs when height limits cause buildings to top out at the same or near same height. It may be a deliberately sought or an unwanted effect depending upon the nature of the city.

ganizing order compounds the chaos of much fringe development. These random forms cannot be easily retrieved or translated into a future state of wholeness and order.

Height limits can cause problems under some circumstances. When high-rise project after project presses against the height limit the resulting benching can be visually damaging in some settings. When benching is not desired, it can be minimized or eliminated simply and directly by avoiding extended horizontal height districts and creating many small and varied districts.

A more exotic approach is treating height district boundaries like

*Existing height limits in downtown
San Francisco, adopted in 1971.*

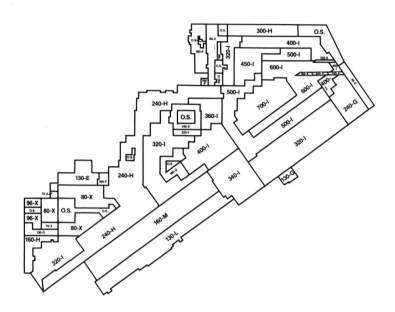

*Proposed height limits for down-
town San Francisco, 1984.*

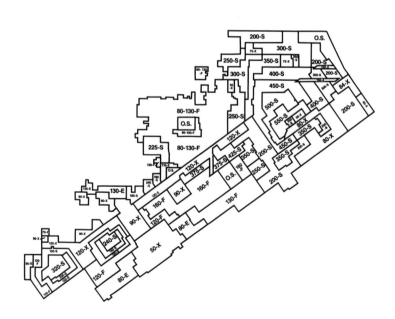

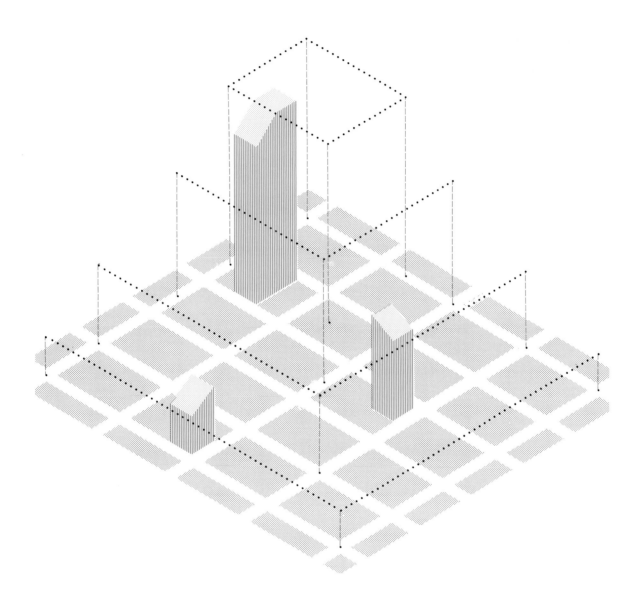

Building height contours would delineate a potential volume the same way land contours describe a hill. At any point, permitted building height would be proportional to the distance between contour lines.

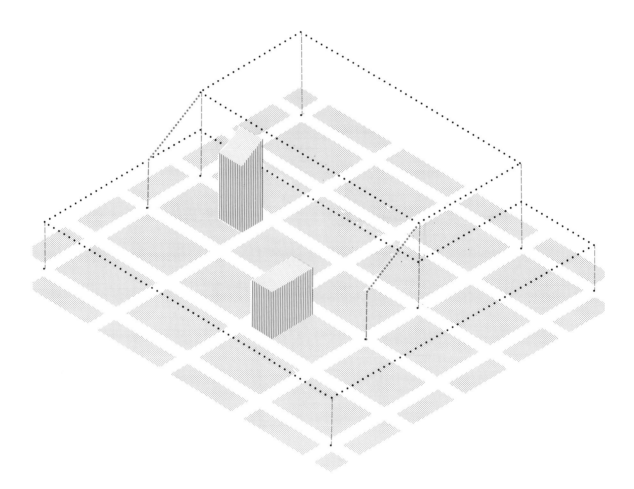

Transitional height zones work in a similar manner as contours but can be applied selectively to standard height districts.

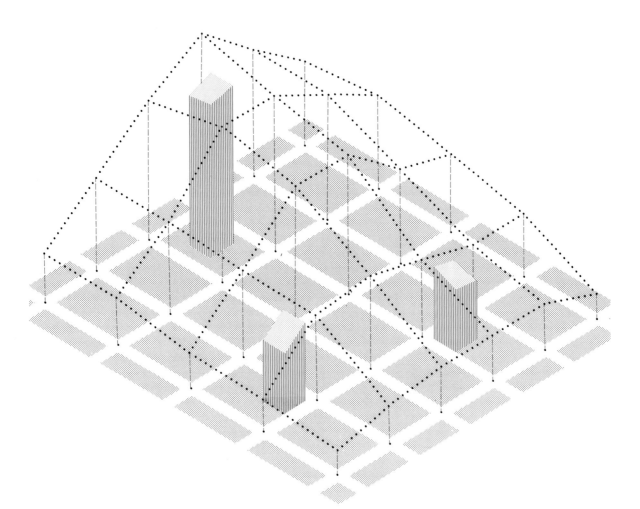

Point net envelope.

118

Variable height extension examples.

A. Added height is not permitted as it would work against the desired stepping.

B. The project is eligible to use the full 10 percent height extension possible as it permits the building to act as a transitional step between adjacent buildings.

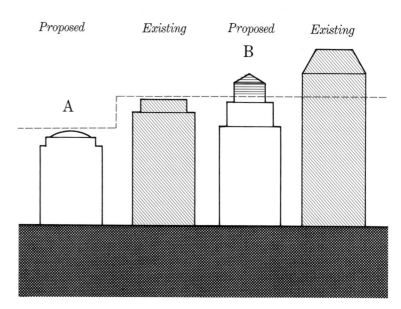

Proposed *Existing* *Proposed* *Existing*

B

A

contour lines, with height graduated between the elevations represented by the lines. Drawing the height contour lines can be difficult in complicated situations, and substantially the same effect can be achieved through the selective application of transitional zones to standard height districts which eliminates many mapping problems. The transitional zones define a tapered height zone eliminating the abrupt step between one district and another except where desired for design reasons.

Even more exotic and geometrically elegant is a point net envelope that defines a volume by elevations set at each street intersection and other points as needed. Connecting scaled lines that extend vertically from these points defines the envelope in terms of triangular or rectangular planes inclined at various angles. To determine exactly how high a developer could go on a given site would entail a bit of detail work that could be a problem if all potential sites were not calculated in advance via an axonometric construct.

Another height control method permits addressing specific contextual form problems that might be encountered using standard height districting. A variable height extension offers the opportunity to increase heights up to a set maximum percentage of total permitted height if the added height meets specific criteria. To obtain the additional height the developer might be required to demonstrate that the added height facilitates a graceful transition, helps achieve a superior contextual design, does not cast any additional shadows on public open space, or whatever urban design issue is pertinent.

Sunlight

Whatever its climatic patterns, every city experiences those perfect days when it is a joy to be outside in the sun and air. A city's public parks, plazas, and playgrounds exist for those special days and any other day that people want to spend outdoors. They are a precious resource that should be protected from building shadows during periods of active use. Sunlight to streets is also a valued urban amenity meriting conservation, although protection may be more varied in application. The need for and the restrictiveness of sunlight controls for streets will reflect local climatic conditions, the size of the city, the uses along the street, and the disposition of public open spaces. A city that endures extended hot weather might actively seek cool, well-shaded streets—in contrast to the protectionist aims of a city with cool, windy summers.

Controls directed toward ensuring sunlight access to streets and open space are a form of height control that can significantly affect urban form. Sunlight angles designed to ensure sunlight to the open space in an area where tall buildings might cast shadows can affect the height of buildings within several blocks, depending on which hours the sunlight is desired. A large bowl of space may have to be carved from potential development around a park or playground to assure adequate sunlight. Existing large buildings may modify the limits imposed, and a project that does not add to the existing shadow pattern does no harm.

An absolute prohibition against casting shade upon a park sounds ideal, but in practice can appear quite foolish considering that even the smallest bungalow casts a fearsomely long shadow in the early morning and late evening hours. For this reason most controls assume a limited amount of shadowing. If it is a formal plaza or square where the need for good spatial definition is crucial, the requirements for solar access may have to be altered accordingly.

The determination of precisely where to draw the line, where to "reasonably" stop slicing off a bit of sunlight here and there before nothing is left can be difficult with or without political pressure. The real issue may be the precedent being set and the systematic erosion of sunlight rather than the specific loss under formal review. A carefully defined working definition of "reasonable" is necessary

A solar fan defines the height limits required to assure sunlight for specified times of the day and year. Prepared by the Environmental Simulation Laboratory, University of California, Berkeley.

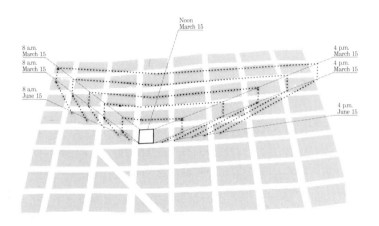

to prevent aggressive architects and developers from translating the vague meaning of that word into an everwidening door. Such a definition should take into account who uses the park, when and how they use it, what areas are most intensively used, and potential future use. An absolute prohibition against any shadowing within the set timeframe avoids difficult, hairsplitting decisions but can also yield some strange and unattractive results.

The height limits for assuring sunlight to open space may be incorporated into the standard height district format, stated as an irregular geometric cone sloping outward from the open space, or translated into level but irregularly shaped steps called a solar fan and mapped as an overlay district. The extent of shadows cast by buildings can be prepared manually using a sun calculator, drawn by a computer for as many time intervals and days as desired, or studied photographically. Plotted shadow patterns have the advantage in that they distinguish new from existing shadows and determine the precise shadow effect on popular gathering points. A thorough survey of how the space is used at different times of the day and year and under differing climatic conditions is invaluable for assessing impact.

A fish-eye view of a city playground with the path of the sun at mid-winter, spring and fall equinoxes, and mid-summer. Note: Solar time and clock time may be at a variance of up to 15 minutes. Prepared by the Environmental Simulation Laboratory, University of California, Berkeley.

A 360-degree fish-eye lens collapses onto the flat surface of a photo everything that can be seen from a given point. The picture, although distorted as in a fun house mirror, will show all the sky and all the buildings visible from that point. Plotting the path of the sun with a solar calculator at various times of the year yields an annual sun time, showing when the sun is visible or blocked by buildings. The part of a building that blocks sunlight access is evident when the sun path is superimposed over the photo, facilitating design adjustments. Because the fish-eye lens only provides a valid picture from a specific point, a number of photo points would be required to explain what is happening generally. The primary advantage is that it reduces to one graphic plate the complex story of the sun's actions over an entire year, providing a framework for interpreting a limited number of static plans with plotted shadows.

While it is eminently wise and sensible to ensure continued sunlight access to parklands, it does not follow that every street should receive similar treatment. A diversity of environmental and spatial experiences is an important part of the richness that cities have to offer. Controls directed at assuring sunlight to the street should integrate a consideration of human needs with the appropriateness of the uses along the street and an eye for pattern and effect. Low-scaled sunny areas and high-rise districts are proper compositional elements to be used in the design of cities. But within downtown areas neither should dominate completely and as a general policy, there should be no more than a five-minute walk from the center of any dense high-rise building cluster to a pleasant sunny open space or an area of relatively small-scaled sunny streets. The best man-made high-rise canyons are dramatic and exciting and never so extended in area that they become prisons. Toward this objective, San Francisco has proposed new height districts that bound the dense working population of the financial district by relatively small-scaled areas and open spaces. The reduced heights proposed in the retail core will protect the special environmental character that has helped make the area one of the most vital retail centers in the nation.

Controlling Sunlight Access

Each method for protecting sunlight access to streets makes a unique imprint on the form and character of the street and cityscape. Individual approaches may also have radically different impacts on the development potential of the abutting land. Examples of the basic tools for controlling sunlight access follow. These tools can be creatively mixed and modified to achieve not only their stated objectives but a surprising palette of urban forms.

Height Limits

The standard building height limit is the most basic mechanism for assuring sunny streets. Either the height can be derived from the sun angle desired or the sun angle can be the by-product of a desired street wall height. This method is not well suited for differentiating between north-south and east-west streets.

Setbacks

Requiring a setback of a certain number of feet at a specified height, when coupled with a height limit, establishes a sun angle the same as a height limit alone. This arrangement differs in two ways: the development potential can be increased while keeping the same street wall height and the setback introduces a layered effect that can strengthen and inject added formality into the streetscape. The tiering of a series of setbacks, each progressively deeper, could be used to create a special streetscape.

Conditional Height

Above a base "by right" height, obtaining additional building height is made conditional on meeting specified criteria for achieving a wide variety of objectives in addition to sunlight contol. Greater height could be permitted if, for example, it did not add to the shadows on public sidewalks between 11 a.m. and 3 p.m.. Additional height also could be tied to parking requirements, building material, color, achievement of a particular image, or design review. The great flexibility possible through the application of performance criteria makes this an attractive design tool.

Sun Angles

Sun angles are designed to assure sunlight to sidewalk areas or other public spaces between selected hours. The angle usually starts at the opposite curb line and defines the street wall height and setbacks up to the maximum height. The angles will vary with the street orientation and width. They may be less restrictive on north-south streets than east-west streets as the angle required to obtain additional minutes of sunlight quickly is limited. Pursued to excess without thought to the form consequences, sun angle requirements could yield a bizarre sawtooth city profile.

View Angles

View angles are primarily intended to maintain a specific visual scale irrespective of the intensity of development behind the facade and require that height exceeding the mandated facade height be hidden from the pedestrian. View angles work much the same as sun angles but usually are more restrictive above the selected facade height. They are very useful for new construction within a historic dictrict where retention of the sense of scale of the district is important.

Tower Spacing

Where high buildings are wanted, the spacing between towers determines how much sunlight can reach the street. Substantial shadowing occurs from the towers themselves, but controls assure that at least intermittent shafts of sunlight reach public areas. Own-

Sun access angles required to assure sunlight six months a year on sidewalks in downtown San Francisco.

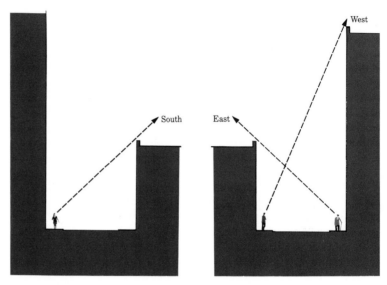

North-South Street   East-West Street

A view angle is that angle of view below which the average pedestrian cannot see construction above and behind a given height facade.

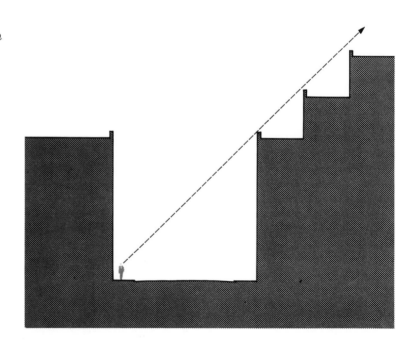

ers have a vested interest in keeping the modern high rise reasonably spaced because of the adverse effect on rents when views are severely constrained. Such controls provide reputable developers and owners a measure of protection.

A building that is many times the width of neighboring buildings may present difficult architectural problems. As the height of the wide building increases above that of its neighbors, the nature of the design problem quickly changes. Articulating the facade is no longer enough to ameliorate the clash in scale. Substantial changes in the mass of the building itself are required to reduce the overwhelming bulk and achieve an agreeable contextual fit.

The elevation at which bulk begins to be an issue is relative to the prevalent height of surrounding development. Above that control

Bulk Controls

Example of a side setback requirement.

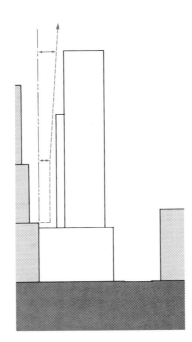

point, the perception of bulk depends on the scale of surrounding buildings and, within limits, the configuration of the upper part of the tower.

The massive U- and E- plan office towers that were popular in the 1920s managed to defuse problems of bulk through the use of small-scaled features and embellishments. Chimneys disguised as temples, corner pavilions, chateau roof forms, gothic spires, and romantic clock towers helped link large bulky buildings to their smaller neighbors. Modern architecture's current strictures largely exclude such devices. A slender top can help offset the massiveness of the lower portions of a building by imparting a sense of lightness and gracefulness to the whole. Effective devices that help diminish the impression of oversized bulk include articulation of the building mass to create the impression of an aggregation of smaller forms, and changes in exterior cladding to disguise the true width (much as costume designers seek to hide the bulk of an overweight prima donna). Each method or combination of methods has its limitations; when pressed to do the impossible, they may merely achieve the ridiculous. Bulk controls are a means for keeping the design problems within the range of available design solutions.

As very wide buildings rise above smaller neighbors, they present increasingly difficult design problems that cannot easily be corrected by minor articulation of the facade.

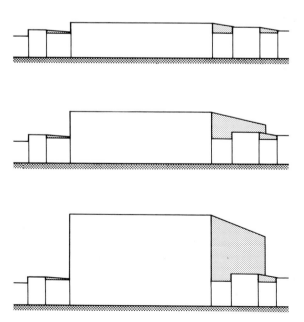

Plan Dimensions

20' × 120'

110' × 120'

200' × 120'

250' × 120'

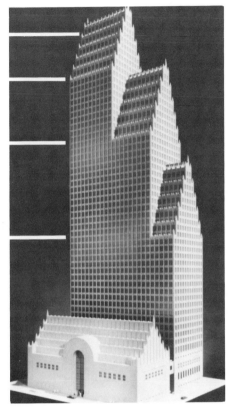

The slender, delicately scaled top of the Republic Bank Center by Johnson/Burgee in Houston imparts a graceful quality to the entire building. The tiered roof form is repeated three times on the tower and once more on the ancillary base building, providing a unit of measure for comprehending the scale of the building and a basis for the individual on the ground to relate to the whole.

Tall bulky buildings pose serious urban design problems in any cityscape. Thin in one dimension and extremely wide in the other, the contemporary slab tower is a particularly awkward building form within the city. Le Corbusier correctly envisioned it standing alone in a parklike setting, not jammed together with other buildings. While the narrow end may be elegantly tall and slender, the broad side is so vast and flat that no other building can relate to it. Box top office towers of great girth also present a looming, overscaled presence out of scale with surrounding development. By themselves they are disruptive and aggregated they can only result in a clumsy, lumpish cityscape.

Some building mass may have to be eliminated or redistributed to bring bulk within the range of reasonable design treatment. The most important place to diminish the size of the building is at the top. A small change from top to bottom is not as effective as concentrating the reduction in a highly visible way at the top, an action not likely to win many friends in the development community.

In the Embarcadero Center in San Francisco, four slab buildings are lined up in a 1,200-foot-long row blocking downtown views to and from Telegraph Hill. They give this extremely sensitive edge of the downtown an unnecessarily blunt, awkward appearance. San Francisco's bulk controls were an effort to prevent further city form abuses of this kind. The widest of these slabs exceeds the maximum width of current controls by 70 feet.

The reason is quite simple; high-rise building owners get more rent per square foot at the top of buildings than at the bottom and this rent differential is why a city has to *require* builders to reduce the size of upper floors.

Bulk limits should not become rigid form constraints, particularly if a high floor area ratio is easy to come by. In efforts to maximize economic return, the developer will seek to pack in as much square footage and build as large a typical floor as is consonant with market demand. Form constraints that limit exterior dimensions press against the developer's objectives and leave little room for the architect to work. Dimensional restraints by themselves can prevent the worst excesses but may also impose an unwanted similarity of form that makes it difficult to obtain the sculpturing needed for a good contextual fit.

Case Study: San Francisco Bulk Controls. The bulk controls San Francisco adopted in 1971 established four maximum bulk envelopes that took effect at different elevations. The heights above which the controls took effect were derived from the typical scale of the different parts of the city to which they were applied.

The 1971 San Francisco Bulk Controls			
Height above which Maximum Dimensions Apply	Length (feet)	Diagonal (feet)	Applicable Areas
40, 50, 80	110	125	Residential
40, 65, 80	110	140	Residential & Fringe Office
80, 100, 150	170	200	Downtown Office
40, 60, 80, 100	250	300	Industrial

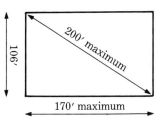

Maximum Rectangle

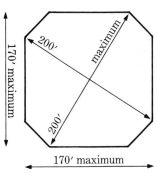

Maximum Polygon

In the downtown area, the maximum length (or width) of 170 feet coupled with a maximum plan diagonal of 200 feet was applied. These maximums translated into a basic rectangle of 170-by-106 feet. The maximum floor size possible within these controlling dimensions was 26,810 square feet. Building after building pressed against the dimensional limits, indicating that had they not existed even more massive buildings would have been built. (When the controls were put in place there were serious rumors that a Chicago-scaled behemoth was being planned. The evidence of the success of the controls is that it was not built.)

Unfortunately, the buildings that were built were still regrettably overscaled forms in the context of the fine background scale of San Francisco. It was not that 170 feet was too large at the bottom or even at middle of the building; it was too large when that measure extended from top to bottom of a high rise. The box top towers lined up on the skyline with all the grace of a refrigerator showroom. The contols limited the maximum dimensions of the refrigerators but did nothing to affect the form of the tower. It should be noted that the bulk controls were not causing the box top shape. Similar buildings were springing up in cities across the nation,and there was a mechanism for excepting the dimensional requirements in return for a better design.

To obtain the form changes needed to make buildings work better with other buildings and within the skyline, it was necessary to forceably wean architects and developers from the deadly box top formula. Controls were needed that would lead architects to design buildings with clearly defined bases, midsections, and tops where the adjustments for achieving a good contextual relationship could fit comfortably into the design.

Maximum Average Floor Areas

The method used sought to combine a desirable degree of flexibility with needed restraint and the least specific design bias. The key was to set maximum *average* floor areas instead of a rigid envelope for the upper portions of the building. Within the midtower and top, some floors could be increased in size if others were correspondingly decreased. Dimensional restraints still were necessary because the maximum average floor area by itself could not prevent the wide thin slabs that were often used in hotels or on odd narrow sites. The maximum facade width was deliberately made larger than required to contain the maximum average floor area and to ensure that the architect was not trapped between form restraints and the developer's desires.

At the maximum possible floor size, approximately the top 25 percent of the total building height would be limited in area to 60 percent of the average floor area of the midtower zone, ensuring that the most visible part of the building would be sympathetic to the scale of smaller downtown buildings. The required reduction of the top average floor area is not limited to the maximum floor sizes. As the average floor size for the midtower zone decreases, a reduction is still required, reducing in amount with the floor size. The percentage of total building height forming the top zone also drops off rapidly below 200 feet in height. The bulk controls are tied to the height of the building, not to the height district.

Expressing the floor sizes in terms of averages gives the designer considerable latitude as to how and where the transition from midtower to top occurs. Opportunity for the further sculpturing of the building top is provided by flexibility in massing mechanical equipment at the building top. Mechanical space must be an integral part of the architecture, not a little box perched on top of the building.

No floor area or dimensional restraints are proposed for the base zone of the building. The one difference from the 1971 controls is that the base height is predicated on the width of the abutting street and not a height set for a zoning district. Random setbacks from

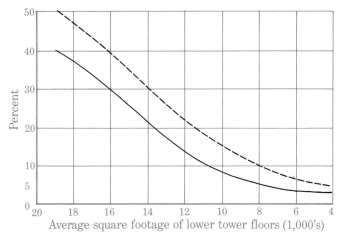

**Percent reduction
in volume of upper tower**
as a result of extension
of the lower tower

Reduction required at or
below the height limit

- - - - - - - - - - - - -
Reduction required with
18% height extension

Upper Tower Reduction

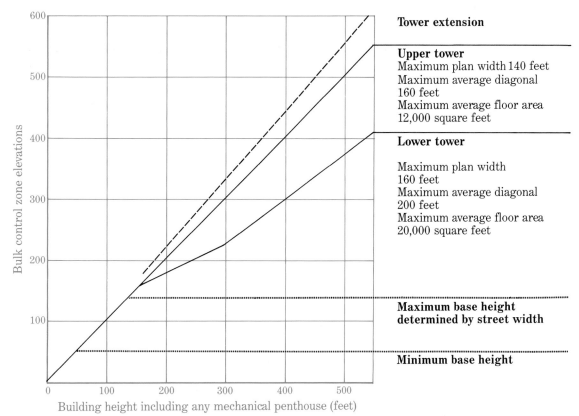

Tower extension

Upper tower
Maximum plan width 140 feet
Maximum average diagonal
160 feet
Maximum average floor area
12,000 square feet

Lower tower

Maximum plan width
160 feet
Maximum average diagonal
200 feet
Maximum average floor area
20,000 square feet

**Maximum base height
determined by street width**

Minimum base height

Bulk control zone elevations

Building height including any mechanical penthouse (feet)

Heights at Which Bulk Controls Take Effect

the property line are discouraged, as are plazas and miscellaneous sidewalk widenings that were previously credited with floor area bonuses under the old zoning controls. Plazas are still possible as a means of meeting required open space. The placement of plazas, however, is carefully controlled to avoid chewing up the traditional street pattern in return for vague ill-defined spaces.

Bulk controls facilitate the improvement of wind conditions at the street level. Tall buildings intercept wind at upper levels and direct

Comparison of Existing and Proposed Bulk Controls.

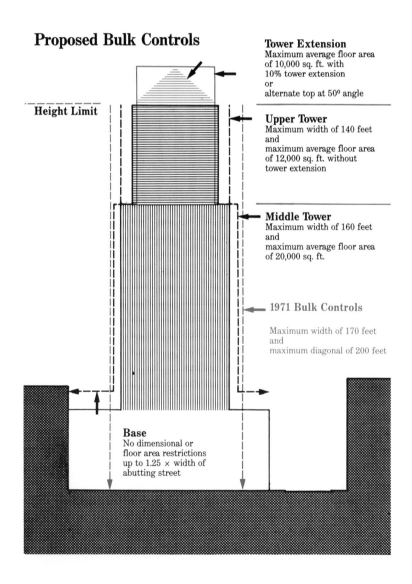

Proposed Bulk Controls

Tower Extension
Maximum average floor area of 10,000 sq. ft. with 10% tower extension
or
alternate top at 50° angle

Height Limit

Upper Tower
Maximum width of 140 feet and
maximum average floor area of 12,000 sq. ft. without tower extension

Middle Tower
Maximum width of 160 feet and
maximum average floor area of 20,000 sq. ft.

1971 Bulk Controls

Maximum width of 170 feet and
maximum diagonal of 200 feet

Base
No dimensional or floor area restrictions up to 1.25 × width of abutting street

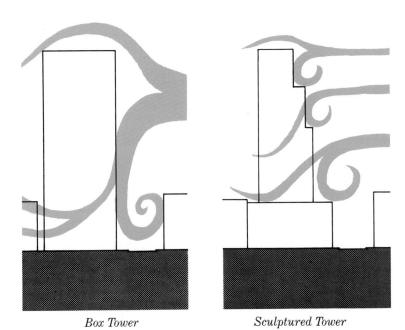

Box Tower   *Sculptured Tower*

some of it downward to the street. The wider the building and the smoother its surface, the stronger building-generated wind turbulence can be at the base. The introduction of building setbacks can reduce this effect by diverting wind flow before it reaches the street. To the degree that bulk controls result in articulated and stepped building forms, they work to decrease wind problems. But bulk controls cannot by themselves be relied upon to solve such problems; wind standards and studies also must be directed toward their solution.

San Francisco's proposed new bulk controls illustrate one approach designed to meet the problems of one city. Each community that seeks to address this issue should do so from the perspective of what is needed locally, not what is being done elsewhere. The controls for San Francisco were tailored for that city and would be appropriate only for other cities with similar problems. There are many possible variations. More zones could be added with decreasing average floor areas, increased height above a specified point could be made contingent on increasing slenderness, roof forms could be specified, or floor size limits could be triggered by the elevation above sea level to create a distinctive horizontal break in the

These four examples illustrate the potential variety of urban forms that building controls can be used to achieve.

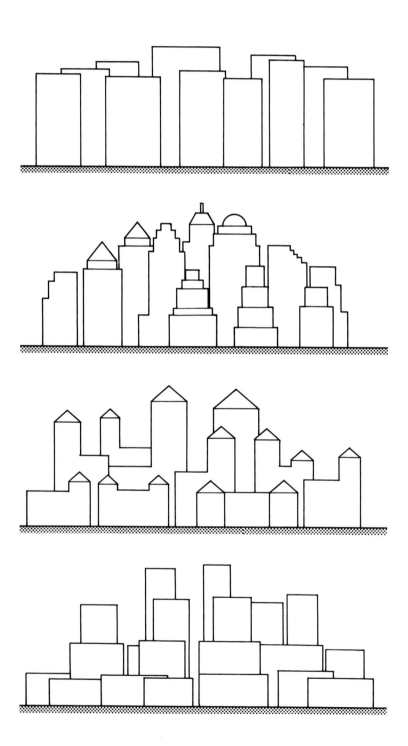

skyline. The combination of bulk and height controls can be used to direct city form and to contribute to a distinctive style and character. Cities need not passively accept the dictates of a bland homogenized development.

DESIGN REVIEW

Short of requiring the builder to copy specific prototypes, it is impossible to legislate good design. No set of rules can anticipate all the situations and conflicts that will eventually surface and there is a tendency that rules designed to prevent something bad will also prevent something good from happening. At best, we stack the odds against the worst and hope for the best. However cleverly the controls have been structured, designers have demonstrated an uncanny ability to technically meet every requirement and still evade the spirit of the underlying design objectives.

Monitoring Quality

Design review can do what controls cannot: monitor the quality of design and the success with which it achieves urban design objectives. The mechanisms for effectuating design review are varied in nature. There is no single correct way; local politics, the size of the community, the pace of development, and the personalities involved will determine what arrangement works best. Design decisions may be made by an independent design commission, an advisory committee to the planning commission, staff, or even by a design review officer with a special range of authority much like that of a zoning administrator. Whatever the process, there are several prerequisites to its most efficient functioning:

• Design objectives should be clearly stated. The developer and architects should know in advance what criteria will be applied to the proposed project.

• The design directions should remain consistent over time. Refinements and minor adjustments are possible but major shifts in character are to be avoided. It may be decades before the effect of some policies can be seen.

• Urban design concerns should provide the primary directions to guide design review. Architecture expresses the design resolution of urban design objectives. Short-term architectural fashions should not be allowed to disrupt long-term planning.

• The basis for exceptions should be clearly spelled out and the rationale open to public scrutiny. It should be difficult to bypass design review by lobbying higher authorities.

• Design review committees should be as small as possible and members holding rigid and divergent architectural beliefs should not be appointed. A small group that shares a vision and has the flexibility to work with a variety of styles will be most effective.

The design review responsibility can be difficult. The design reviewer can avoid risk and possible public embarrassment by restricting comments to the most general statements and never making a specific recommendation. By keeping public comments suitably vague and oracular, he can appear quite intelligent and responsible and never let himself be caught in a bad decision. A smoke screen of architectural bafflegab (the dominant architectural language) can be an excellent defensive position from which to turn down a design without danger of counterattack. But design proposals can be turned down only so many times before the architect can loudly claim he is being treated unfairly and that he can do what is wanted if only someone will tell him what that is. No-risk design review—sometimes referred to as the "I'll know the answer when I see it" approach—may be good for the reviewer but it is not fair to the architect or the developer and it will not yield good urban design.

A preferable approach is to have the design reviewers involved in the process at least to the extent of identifying and defining the design problems as clearly as possible and pointing out possible avenues for solving them. Sometimes the particular stylistic approach selected by the designer will not solve the design problems and must be changed. In most cases, the issue can be resolved within the selected design vocabulary. Designers respond well to a discussion of the principles involved in resolving specific design problems drawn from successful solutions by other—not necessarily living—architects. When proposed, a given approach should take into consideration the designer's limitations, and the recommended design language or style should be equal to the designer's skills. It is important that the recommended approach can yield a successful solution. The idea first should be tested with paper and pencil unless a workable prototype exists—just because an approach sounds plausible does not mean the words can be translated into acceptable architecture.

Tangible Design

There is a vast gulf between words and designs. The designer's description of the visual impact of the design shouldn't deserve too much attention: If how the design relates to surrounding buildings must be explained, the relationship may not exist except in a technical or intellectual sense. There will not be a bronze plaque out front explaining how the design relates to its context; it must be self-evident. Reality is more important than words and concepts. Buildings must speak for themselves. Attention is warranted when the architect describes how the building functions and the materials and colors he plans to use, but the philosophical diatribes and dreamy word pictures of how wonderful it is going to be can be ignored. It is, however, important to try to picture just how it will look in 10 or 20 years when it is no longer new and shining and the stylistic enthusiasms of the moment have long vanished.

No matter how involved the reviewer may become in the design process the design is still in the hands of the architect representing his client. For better or worse, the architect will develop and refine the project. If the reviewer's concept is used but executed poorly, the concept is still his. If that aspect of the building attracts public attention, the reviewer may find himself saddled with the blame. That is the risk of becoming involved, but the risk is worth it if it purchases stronger and more clearly articulated urban design concepts.

Presentation Methods

The foundation of good design review is understanding the future reality of the proposal. The reviewer makes his decisions based on elevations, sketches, models, axonometric drawings, etc. Each method can distort the proposal and mislead the viewer in a different way, so that awareness of the shortcomings of the media being used is absolutely essential. Sometimes a misdirection is intentional; just as often the designer is also confusing graphics with reality. It is very instructive to check the accuracy of one's vision of what-is-to-be against the reality of the completed project. The serious reviewer will soon learn to distrust all presentation material and to always ask, "What will this really look and feel like?"

Such presentation material may include the following forms of design information:

Elevations

Elevations translate a three-dimensional design into a two-dimensional statement, presenting a view impossible to obtain in the real world. By themselves they are inadequate for evaluating a design. The viewer is given little basis for evaluating the three-dimensional strength of the design, and only his imagination can produce a real world view.

Line drawings of elevations mislead because the lines invariably are stronger visually than the joints and edges they represent. The combined effect of the lines on a small scale yields a relatively dense pattern that is viewed all at once but at full scale the pattern is stretched out and thin. Many lines simply disappear at the distance required to see the entire building. Close in the overall pattern may not be seen and if relatively flat, the viewer will get little sense of the rhythm.

Shadows help in understanding the three-dimensional qualities of a facade; however, they do tend to overstate the effect. The application of solid black shadows to the elevation is frequently a signal that the design is so dull that it needed a little tarting up. Sharp, intense shadows are often used to make unremarkable sculpturing appear more significant.

Perspective Drawings

Perspectives provide the three-dimensional information elevations lack, but lines will mislead in the same way. Few artists can successfully convey a true sense of mass and texture. The more common problem of perspective drawings is that the artist and the developer tend to present the building from that one point from which it looks the most dramatic, regardless of the practicality of that point of view. The viewpoint may float many floors above the ground or be possible only by the convenient invisibility of intervening buildings. The corner of the building may slice through the air with the drama of a ship's prow. Banners can fly above with baroque grandeur while the shadows of passing clouds dramatically pattern the brilliant sparkling facade. To complete the picture a little girl—startled by a flock of doves—will have lost her balloon which is floating up past the color coordinated banners. All these features may be fine for selling prospective tenants, but they are irrelevant to the design and get in the way of thoughtful design review. Reliability is the main problem with perspective drawings; it is too easy to misinform on a grand scale. Rendering tricks can disguise a clumsy, leaden design concept, misrepresent the true scale, and suggest a happy addition to the surrounding buildings.

Axonometric View

Axonometric drawings are useful for showing the massing of a building relative to surrounding structures. They mislead in that the viewer is always placed high in the air where few, if any, people will ever see the design. They place undue emphasis on the roof and exaggerate the effect of the sculpturing of the building mass, making certain kinds of massing appear significant when they are actually invisible from the ground.

Models

Models are valuable in appraising designs. There is little distortion of the massing effect when they are used properly, and they enable the viewer to examine the project in context from many angles. The problem with models is that they make things look cute; in miniature, a steel mill or a freeway will seem cute as a bug. An eight-lane freeway becomes a serene exercise in elegant geometrics and extended blank walls shed their Kafkaesque qualities.

At a small scale, models, like drawings, can condense designs and imply a richness that in fact will not exist. Technical limitations in replicating scale detailing result in their exaggeration; joints between panels become a striking aspect of the facade, and blandness is transformed into visual spice. Rough cardboard models can suggest a strength and vigor that is derived from the pebbly surface of the board, exposed edges, and deliberately sketchy workmanship that the built project will never possess. Because the best models of their kind are works of art, an art unrelated to reality, it is necessary for the viewer to discount the effects and envision a more accurate reality. When models are the primary method of display their use invariably leads to the Mt. Olympus syndrome, that is, the model sits on a table and everyone stands looking down at it. Even if the viewer makes a point of getting down on one knee and carefully studying the project from scale eye level, most of the time will be spent looking down at it. That view easily becomes the dominant impression, which heightens the importance of aspects that are not important from the ground at the expense of those that are.

A one inch per 50 feet scale is adequate for studying a project's

Photomontage of original proposal indicated that the project would present a wide slab effect from east and west views along the street. Sculpturing at top had little effect from the side. Floor area ratio of 14:1.

Revised design equally sculptures top in both directions. Top design that appeared vigorous in the model looks oddly blunted from a pedestrian's point of view. Floor area ratio of 14:1.

142

Silhouette of an approved project is now indicated in foreground. Project has been reduced from F.A.R. 14:1 to 10:1 to meet proposed downtown controls. The cone on top does not seem to grow out of the tower and the stepping on sides seems somewhat abrupt.

Revised design ties the top and the rest of building together through repetition of same angled plane. The stepping on the sides also is more graceful.

Photomontages were prepared by Square One Film + Video for Lincoln Properties. H.O.K. Architects.

massing in the context of adjacent buildings. For evaluating urban open spaces and facades as part of the streetscape, the larger the scale the better; one-half inch per foot is usually satisfactory.

Photomontage

Photomontage offers one of the best ways to evaluate the design of a building within its context. It requires a highly detailed model of sufficient size to make the detailing appear realistic and a careful match of the angle and distance used to photograph the project site. The very best photomontage work eliminates the "new building effect," giving the impression of a real building that has been in place a number of years. Photomontage can be a valuable design tool to the architect, permitting the design to be seen in a real world context from typical points of view and helping eliminate the contemporary designer's tendency to conceptualize in the abstract by introducing reality to ideas that have little to do with experience.

NOTES ON AN URBAN DESIGN EDUCATION

Universities each year churn out an army of would-be architects and, having thought better of it, also produce a small squad of would-be urban designers to prevent the architects from doing too much damage. To make certain the virus and antibodies do not mix beforehand, urban design is tucked away in city planning schools, where few architectural students are likely to stumble across it. To the degree that urban design is something that city planners do to architects and developers, placement under the city planning umbrella makes sense.

But treating urban design as something separate and discrete from architecture is a serious error. It tells the architectural student that urban design is a responsibility of others, not architects. It says that urban design is not a function of architecture but rather of planning. This is made confusing by the assertion that planning is a process, a highly intangible element unlikely to produce any visible product itself.

Putting urban design education within city planning schools further gives students the impression that urban designers do not need particularly strong architectural skills. Students who are weak in design but still want to have a hand in important design decisions tend to view urban design as an honorable haven from the ego-shredding demands of architecture. There is some truth to this. There is room in urban design for people without a strong sense of design to the degree that urban designers function as cherry pickers: "Hmm. This is good. Hmm. That is bad." Some architectural offices work the same way. Many architects rise to leadership positions more on their social skills than design capability and never come near a drafting table. But just as there is room for only a few front office architects there are similar limitations on urban designers.

There is a need for urban designers with strong design skills. The urban designer must be able to spot the design deficiencies and also point the way toward and define the parameters of a successful solution. Before the urban designer says, "Do this!" he must be certain it is correct.

There is very little of a design-related nature relevant to urban design that an architect should not also know. Every architect should regard urban design as a function of architecture, an integral part of the design problem to be resolved. For effective urban design the debate must shift from the need and importance of defining street space and scale, for example, to how strongly it should be defined. The difference between the urban design and the architecture must become merely a matter of scale and time, not substance.

If an architect or urban designer were given the assignment to determine how best to improve the architectural quality of a city, the first step would be to identify the architecturally meritorious buildings. He would suffer peculiar problems if unable to distinguish a significant building from one lacking in merit, but it is no exaggeration that many architects today suffer from this problem. An architect hired to assist in a citywide survey proved incapable of seeing any excellence or aesthetic value in *any* structure with decorative detail, irrespective of style. Only a very few bare stucco box houses met his exacting standards. Due to the strength of design prejudices acquired at school, it proved impossible to convince this man that Italianate Flatfronts, voluptuous Queen Annes, Shingle Style, or Spanish Revival had any merit at all.

Wearing similar intellectual blinders, architects are deciding every day not to relate new designs to adjacent buildings they consider unworthy. Participation in an architectural survey requiring the evaluation of buildings in dozens and dozens of different style categories is a marvelous eye opener. It forces the surveyor to look beyond stylistic preferences and prejudices and see those design relationships that give buildings their quality, or lack thereof. In the process, the surveyor is exposed to a wealth of design solutions.

Urban designers must work with many different kinds of architects; architects must design buildings in many different contexts. Both need to be able to think and work in a variety of design languages or styles. To students, the requirement to design projects in a variety of styles provides rich resources to expand personal design skills. The in-depth exposure to the work of historic architects can only strengthen the resourcefulness of the young designer trying to cope with contemporary fashions. Along with this there is a crying need to make everyone aware of the illusions that lie in fashionable presentation techniques and to acquire the skill to envision the buildings as they will really appear.

Many architectural schools are reluctant to deny a diploma to students poor at design. They recognize that many jobs in architecture demand other skills that do not often accompany those of design. Then too, architects are notorious late bloomers in design. For some, their skills as a designer only begin to shine after many years of plodding. But what about those who never bloom, never shine, and do a lot of unnecessary damage in the process? The missing ingredient in these lesser lights of the design professions appears to be a basic inability to differentiate good from better. Design judgment can exist independent of the ability to design. Architectural historians and critics who might not be able to design the inside of a hall closet may enjoy an exceptional acuity of design perception. These are talents that can be tested with some reliability. It would seem to be far easier to deny entrance into a design school on the basis of a carefully crafted test of aesthetic judgment than to deny a diploma after several years of hard work. It will not weed out those who do not care, but could reduce the numbers of those who are unable to bring the necessary vision to the job.